Financial performance

Workbook

second edition

Aubrey Penning

osborne
BOOKS

Published by Osborne Books Limited
Unit 1B Everoak Estate
Bromyard Road
Worcester WR2 5HP
Tel 01905 748071
Email books@osbornebooks.co.uk
Website www.osbornebooks.co.uk

Design by Laura Ingham
Cover and page design image © Istockphoto.com/Petrovich9

Printed and bound in Great Britain by CPI Group (UK) Ltd, Croydon, CR0 4YY

British Library Cataloguing in Publication Data
A catalogue record for this book is available from the British Library

ISBN 978 1905777 846

Contents

Chapter activities

Chapter activities – answers

Practice assessments

Practice assessments – answers

Acknowledgements

The authors wish to thank the following for their help with the production of the book: Maz Loton, Jon Moore and Cathy Turner. Thanks are also due to Lynn Watkins for her technical editing and to Laura Ingham for her designs for this new series.

The publisher is indebted to the Association of Accounting Technicians for its kind permission to reproduce sample practice assessment material.

Author

Aubrey Penning has many years experience of teaching accountancy on a variety of courses in Worcester and Gwent. He is a Certified Accountant, and before his move into full-time teaching he worked for the health service, a housing association and a chemical supplier. Until recently he was the AAT course coordinator at Worcester College of Technology, specialising in the areas of management accounting and taxation.

Introduction

what this book covers

This book has been written specifically to cover the Learning Area 'Financial Performance' which covers two QCF Units in the AAT Level 4 Diploma in Accounting:

■ Principles of managing financial performance

■ Measuring financial performance

what this book contains

This book is set out in two sections:

■ **Chapter activities** which provide extra practice material in addition to the activities included in the Osborne Books Tutorial text. Answers to the Chapter activities are set out in this book.

■ **Practice Assessments** are included to prepare the student for the Computer Based Assessments. They are based directly on the structure, style and content of the sample assessment material provided by the AAT at www.aat.org.uk. Suggested answers to the Practice Assessments are set out in this book.

online support from Osborne Books

This book is supported by practice material available at www.osbornebooks.co.uk

This material is available to tutors – and to students at their discretion – in two forms:

■ A **Tutor Zone** which is available to tutors who have adopted the Osborne Books texts. This area of the website provides extra assessment practice material (plus answers) in addition to the activities included in this Workbook text.

■ **Online learning** – online practice questions designed to familiarise students with the style of the AAT Computer Based Assessments.

Scan the code on the right using your Smartphone to gain access to the online practice questions.

further information

If you want to know more about our products, please visit www.osbornebooks.co.uk, email books@osbornebooks.co.uk or telephone Osborne Books Customer Services on 01905 748071.

Chapter activities

Chapter activities
Management accounting techniques

1.1 The table below contains the last three months cost per kilogram for product Alpha.

January	February	March
Actual price was £20.40	Actual price was £19.20	Actual price was £21.00
Seasonal variation was +£1.20	Seasonal variation was -£0.30	Seasonal variation was +£1.20

The trend in prices is an increase of £ _____ per month.

1.2 A company has provided the following information:

	January	February	March
Total cost	£150,000	£168,000	£225,000
Total quantity purchased	10,000 kg	10,500 kg	12,500 kg

The cost index for March based upon January being the base period of 100 is:

		✓
(a)	150	
(b)	125	
(c)	120	
(d)	83	

1.3 The cost per unit of a product has increased from £50 in January to £54 in April. The cost per unit was £40 when the index was rebased to 100.

✓

(a) The cost index in April was 135 and the increase from January to April is 8.0%	
(b) The cost index in April was 108 and the increase from January to April is 8.0%	
(c) The cost index in April is 125 and the increase from January to April is 35.0%	
(d) The cost index in April is 135 and the increase from January to April is 4.0%	

1.4 Analyse the following features based on whether they apply to marginal costing or absorption costing by ticking the appropriate column in the table.

✓

Feature	Marginal Costing	Absorption Costing
Can be used to set a minimum selling price		
Complies with standard IAS 2 for inventory valuation		
Can be used for planning and control but is of limited use for decision making		
Can be used in conjunction with break-even analysis		
Can be used in conjunction with 'full cost plus' pricing		
Is often used in conjunction with discounted cash flow decision making techniques		

1.5   Avid Greene is considering installing a rainwater recycling system in his house. The system will cost £8,000 to purchase and install. The system would result in an annual saving of £200 in water charges. Avid intends to sell his house in 5 years, and estimates that having a rainwater recycling system will add £5,000 to the sale proceeds of the house. Avid's cost of capital is 10%, and this rate has been used for the discount factors in the table shown below.

(a)   Complete the following table to calculate the net present value of the system.

Year	Detail	Cash Flow £	Discount Factor	Present Value £
0	Purchase and Installation		1.000	
1	Savings and increased house sale proceeds		0.909	
2			0.826	
3			0.751	
4			0.683	
5			0.621	
Net Present Value				

(b)   Complete the following sentence.

The net present value of the scheme is **positive / negative** so from a financial point of view the scheme is **worthwhile / not worthwhile**.

1.6   The costs for a product have been calculated as follows based on two possible production levels:

Volume of production	10,000 units	18,000 units
Total cost	£100,000	£152,000

Costs are either fixed or variable.

Using the high-low method, estimate the total fixed costs and the variable costs per unit.

1.7   The costs for a product have been calculated as follows based on two possible production levels:

Volume of production	22,000 units	28,000 units
Total cost	£500,000	£606,000

It has been established that the fixed cost element contains a step of £40,000 when volume exceeds 26,000 units. Other costs are variable.

Using the high-low method, estimate the total stepped fixed costs at each production level and the variable costs per unit.

2 Chapter activities
Standard costing – direct costs

2.1 A company purchases 12,000 kilograms of material at a cost of £37,800. The standard cost per kilogram is £3.20. The total material price variance is:

	✓
(a) £0.05 Adverse	
(b) £0.05 Favourable	
(c) £600 Adverse	
(d) £600 Favourable	

2.2 A company used 15,000 kilograms of material at a cost of £37,500. The production was 1000 units, for which the standard usage is 14,500 kilograms of material at a total standard cost of £37,700. The material usage variance is:

	✓
(a) 500 kilograms Adverse	
(b) £1,300 Adverse	
(c) £1,250 Adverse	
(d) £200 Favourable	

2.3 A company expects to produce 18,000 units of Z using 6,000 labour hours. The standard cost of labour is £15 per hour. If the actual output is 17,500 units, what is the standard labour cost for this output?

	✓
(a) £87,500	
(b) £90,000	
(c) £787,500	
(d) £810,000	

2.4 Radnor Ltd manufactures heating equipment. The company has several divisions including the Radiators Division. You work as an Accounting Technician reporting to the Finance Director.

The Radiators Division operates a standard cost system in which:

■ Purchases of materials are recorded at standard cost

■ Direct material and direct labour costs are variable

■ Production overheads are fixed and absorbed on a labour hours basis

The budgeted activity and actual results for the month of November 20-3 are as follows:

	Budget		Actual	
Production units (radiators)		10,000		11,500
Direct materials (paint)	500 litres	£2,500	650 litres	£3,120
Direct material (sheet steel)	30,000 sq metres	£45,000	35,000 sq metres	£51,200
Direct labour	4,000 hours	£48,000	4,100 hours	£51,250
Fixed overheads		£120,000		£120,000
Total cost		£215,500		£225,570

Calculate the following variances for November:

Variance	£	A/F
Direct material (paint) price variance		
Direct material (sheet steel) usage variance		
Direct labour rate variance		
Direct labour efficiency variance		

2.5 A material actually costs £15,400 for 11,500 kg. This results in a favourable material price variance of £700.

All the 11,500 kg purchased were used to make 24,000 units. This resulted in a favourable material usage variance of £700.

(a) The standard material cost per kg is   £

(b) The standard quantity of material to make one unit is   kg

(c) The standard cost of the materials to make one unit is   £

2.6 The direct labour efficiency variance has been accurately calculated for the production of 2,000 units in week 9 as £450 Adverse.

The production took 445 hours. The labour standard time to make one unit is 12 minutes.

The standard time to make 2,000 units is   hours.

The standard labour rate is   £   per hour.

2.7 The actual cost of 5,500 hours of direct labour is £59,400. The direct labour rate variance is £1,100 favourable.

The standard hourly rate is   £   per hour.

2.8 The standard direct material cost is based on using 0.5 kilos of material at £65 per kilo for every unit manufactured.

3,000 units were manufactured, using 1,560 kilos of material with a total cost of £99,840.

Prepare a reconciliation of the budgeted material cost with the actual material cost using the following table.

Budgeted / Standard cost of materials for actual production			
Variances	**Favourable**	**Adverse**	
Direct material price			
Direct material usage			
Total variance			
Actual cost of materials for actual production			

2.9 The standard direct labour time is based on taking 6 hours to make each 100 manufactured units. The standard labour rate is £12.50 per hour.

5,000 units were manufactured, taking 307 labour hours with a total cost of £3,945.

Prepare a reconciliation of the budgeted labour cost with the actual labour cost using the following table.

Budgeted / Standard cost of labour for actual production			
Variances	**Favourable**	**Adverse**	
Direct labour rate			
Direct labour efficiency			
Total variance			
Actual cost of labour for actual production			

3   Chapter activities
Standard costing – fixed overheads

3.1   The following information has been calculated for the production of 1 unit of Zed

- Each unit will require 12 kilograms of material at a cost of £8.50 per kilogram
- Each unit will require 0.6 hours of labour at a total cost of £9
- Fixed overheads total £200,000 and the estimated output will be 2,500 units of Zed
- Fixed overheads are absorbed on a per unit basis

Complete the standard cost card below.

1 unit of Zed	Quantity	Cost per unit £	Total cost £
Material			
Labour			
Fixed costs			
Total			

3.2   You have been given the following information:

- Budgeted overheads are £700,000
- Budgeted output is 35,000 units
- Actual output is 30,000 units
- Actual overheads are £680,000

The fixed overhead volume variance is £ ☐ **favourable / adverse**.

The fixed overhead expenditure variance is £ ☐ **favourable / adverse.**

3.3 You have been given the following information:

- Budgeted overheads are £80,000

- Budgeted output is 10,000 units and 5,000 labour hours

- Actual output is 8,000 units and 4,300 actual labour hours

- Actual overheads are £85,000

The fixed overhead efficiency variance is £ [   ] **favourable / adverse**.

The fixed overhead capacity variance is £ [   ] **favourable / adverse**.

3.4 You have been given the following information:

- Budgeted overheads are £120,000

- Budgeted output is 12,000 units and 4,000 labour hours

- Actual output is 11,400 units and 3,950 actual labour hours

- Actual overheads are £118,000

Complete the following table to show the fixed overhead variances.

	Variance £	A / F	Variance £	A / F
Expenditure Variance				
Capacity Variance				
Efficiency Variance				
Volume Variance				
Total Fixed Overhead Variances				

3.5 Complete the following table by ticking the relevant column to show whether each statement is true or false.

✓

		True	False
(a)	The fixed overhead volume variance will always be numerically equal and opposite to the fixed overhead expenditure variance		
(b)	The fixed overhead capacity variance together with the fixed overhead efficiency variance will always equal the fixed overhead volume variance		
(c)	Adverse variances will be credited to the income statement, while favourable variances will be debited		
(d)	The net total of the fixed overhead expenditure variance and the fixed overhead volume variance is the amount of under or over absorption of fixed overheads		
(e)	If fixed overheads are absorbed on a per unit basis then neither the fixed overhead capacity or efficiency variances can be calculated in the normal way		
(f)	If fixed overheads are absorbed on a direct labour hour basis, then the fixed overhead capacity and efficiency variances will relate to the utilisation of direct labour		

3.6 You have been given the following information:

- Fixed overheads are budgeted at £430,000
- Output is budgeted at 344,000 units
- Fixed overheads are absorbed on a per unit basis
- Actual fixed overheads amount to £419,500
- Actual output is 350,000 units

Prepare a reconciliation of budgeted fixed overheads with actual fixed overheads using fixed overhead variances in the following table.

Budgeted / Standard fixed cost for actual production			
Variances	**Favourable**	**Adverse**	
Fixed overhead expenditure			
Fixed overhead volume			
Total variance			
Actual fixed cost for actual production			

4 Chapter activities
Standard costing – further analysis

4.1 A company bottles cleaning fluid which is sold in two-litre plastic bottles.

The following budgetary control report has been provided:

	Budget		Actual	
Production (bottles)		10,000		10,500
Liquid cleaner	20,000 litres	£25,000	21,100 litres	£25,400
Plastic bottles	10,000 units	£2,000	10,800 units	£2,064
Direct labour	200 hours	£3,300	230 hours	£3,625
Fixed overheads		£7,000		£7,500
Total cost		£37,300		£38,589

The following variances have been accurately calculated, although for some it is not known whether they are adverse or favourable:

Fixed overhead expenditure	£500
Direct materials (liquid cleaner) price	£975 F
Direct materials (bottles) price	£96 F
Direct materials (liquid cleaner) usage	£125 A
Direct materials (bottles) usage	£60
Direct labour rate	£170
Direct labour efficiency	£330 A
Fixed overhead volume	£350 F

Complete the operating statement on the next page, including the budgeted cost for the 10,500 units of production and the variances. Make sure that the total agrees with the actual cost of production.

Budgeted cost for actual production			
Variances:	Favourable	Adverse	
Direct materials (liquid cleaner) price			
Direct materials (liquid cleaner) usage			
Direct materials (bottles) price			
Direct materials (bottles) usage			
Direct labour rate			
Direct labour efficiency			
Fixed overhead expenditure			
Fixed overhead volume			
Total variances			
Actual cost of actual production			

4.2   Aye Limited uses Standard Costing to manage its costs, and absorbs fixed overheads using direct labour hours as an absorption base. It makes one product, and each unit takes five standard direct labour hours to manufacture.

Standard Direct Costs for one unit are:

- ■   Direct Material   3 litres at £4.00 per litre = £12.00 per unit

- ■   Direct Labour   5 hours at £10 per hour = £50.00 per unit

- ■   Fixed Overheads   5 hours at £50 per hour = £250.00 per unit

The standard fixed overheads for one month are £62,500. The standard production output for one month is 1,250 standard hours (i.e. 250 units of product). This gave a budgeted standard absorption rate of £50 per standard direct labour hour as shown above.

During February, actual production was 1,300 standard direct labour hours (i.e. 260 units of product).

Actual Costs for February were as follows:

- ■   Direct Material   800 litres, costing a total of £3,120

- ■   Direct Labour   1,340 hours, costing a total of £14,000

- ■   Fixed Overheads   actual cost £64,800

Calculate and insert all the variances listed in the following table. Use the table to reconcile the budgeted cost of actual production with the actual cost.

Budgeted cost for actual production			
Variances:	Favourable	Adverse	
Direct materials price			
Direct materials usage			
Direct labour rate			
Direct labour efficiency			
Fixed overhead expenditure			
Fixed overhead capacity			
Fixed overhead efficiency			
Total variances			
Actual cost of actual production			

4.3   A company uses material M in its production of product P. Material M has a standard price of £20 per kilo, and a standard usage of 10 kilos per unit of P.

In June, 1,500 units of P were made, using 14,880 kilos of material M.

Since the standards were originally set the specification for manufacturing product P has been amended, resulting in 3% less quantity of material M being required in each unit.

Complete the following table to show the direct material usage variance, and its analysis into the part caused by the change in product specification and the remainder.

Direct Material Usage Variance			Part of variance caused by change in product specification			Part of variance caused by unknown factors		
	£	A / F		£	A / F		£	A / F

4.4   Chippum Limited makes frozen potato chips from raw potatoes that are purchased from UK farms. The potatoes are first machine washed, and then put through a peeling and slicing machine where the chips are cut to shape. At this stage a quality check is carried out by staff who manually pick out from the conveyor system and discard any chips that have blemishes. The chips are then cooked, frozen and bagged ready for sale.

The company operates a standard costing system, and in September the following variances were recorded.

Variance	Adverse £	Favourable £
Direct material (potato) price variance	5,500	
Direct material (potato) usage variance	9,300	
Direct labour rate variance	1,200	
Direct labour efficiency variance	5,600	
Fixed overhead expenditure variance	1,000	
Fixed overhead volume variance	7,400	

The following information has been obtained about the operations during September.

- The recent weather has resulted in a poor potato harvest in the UK. The consequences include higher prices due to shortages as well as poorer quality potatoes with more blemishes than usual.

- The manual quality control operation involved increased hours and overtime working.

- The conveyor system was slowed to enable the more intensive quality control, and this caused mechanical problems, resulting in a break down which lasted several hours. A contractor was used to supply and fit the necessary replacement parts.

Write an email to the Production Director that suggests possible reason(s) for each of the variances, based on the information provided.

| **email** |
| to: |
| from: |
| date: |
| subject: |

4.5   A company uses standard marginal costing to monitor and control its costs. The company's only product is a high energy drink which is purchased in bulk and sold in 500ml cans. The drink, cans and direct labour are all variable costs. Fixed overheads are the only fixed costs.

The following budgetary control report has been provided:

	Budget		Actual	
Production (cans)		6,000,000		5,850,000
Drink	3,000,000 litres	£630,000	2,930,000 litres	£644,600
Cans	6,000,000 units	£240,000	5,855,000 units	£234,200
Direct labour	3,000 hours	£36,000	2,900 hours	£34,500
Fixed overheads		£200,000		£203,500
Total costs		£1,070,000		£1,116,800

Calculate all the variances required and use them to complete the following operating statement.

Budgeted / Standard variable cost for actual production			
Budgeted fixed costs			
Variances	Favourable	Adverse	
Direct materials (drink) price			
Direct materials (drink) usage			
Direct materials (cans) price			
Direct materials (cans) usage			
Direct labour rate			
Direct labour efficiency			
Fixed overhead expenditure			
Total variance			
Actual cost of actual production			

5   Chapter activities
Measuring quality

5.1 Bullseye Limited uses target costing when developing new products. A new product is being considered which has the following cost and revenue information.

Sales   the demand is expected to average 5,000 units per month at a selling price of £7.00 per unit

Materials   the product requires 0.5 kg of material T for each unit

Labour   each unit requires 6 minutes of labour at £14 per hour

Overheads   the product would be manufactured in a separate factory, with total fixed production overheads of £10,000 per month

Profit   the gross margin required is at least 25%

Complete the following table.

Maximum production cost per unit	£
Build up of maximum production cost per unit:	
Materials	£
Labour	£
Overheads	£
Maximum cost per kilo for material T	£

5.2 Delta Limited will be replacing some vans in the next year and needs to decide whether to purchase or lease the vehicles.

The discount factors you will need are shown below.

Year	Discount factor	Year	Discount factor
0	1.00	3	0.864
1	0.952	4	0.823
2	0.907		

(a) Calculate the discounted lifecycle cost of purchasing each van based upon the following:

- Purchase price of £15,000
- Maintenance costs of £800 for each of the next four years, paid annually in arrears
- A residual value of £4,000 at the end of the four years

Year	0	1	2	3	4
Cash flow					
Discount factor					
Present value					
Net present cost					

(b) Calculate the discounted lifecycle cost of leasing each van for four years based upon the total annual costs of £4,100 paid annually in advance. This figure includes maintenance. There is no residual value if leased.

Year	0	1	2	3	4
Lease costs					
Discount factor					
Present value					
Net present cost					

(c) Based on the calculations it is best to **purchase / lease** each van, which saves a net present amount of

£

5.3 Delta Limited is considering designing a new product, and will use target costing to arrive at the target cost of the product. You have been given the following information and asked to calculate the target cost for materials so that the purchasing manager can use this as a target in her negotiations with suppliers.

- The price at which the product will be sold is £40

- The company has firm orders for 10,000 units at a price of £40 for the first year

- The fixed costs are £120,000 per year

- The labour requirement is 20 minutes at a cost of £18 per hour

- The required profit margin is 45%

- The material requirement is 200 grams per unit

(a) Calculate the target cost per kilogram for the materials component of the product, using the following table.

	£
Sales price per unit	
Profit margin	
Total costs	
Fixed cost per unit	
Labour cost per unit	
Maximum material cost per unit	
Target cost per kilogram	

(b) Complete the following statement:

The trade price quoted on the supplier's price list is £25 per kilogram. The purchasing manager has negotiated a discount of 15%. The discount should be **accepted / rejected** because the £25 reduces to £_____ which is **above / below** the Target cost.

(c) The minimum percentage discount needed to achieve the Target cost is [   ] %

5.4 Analyse each of the following cost examples into the four main groups of the cost of quality by ticking the appropriate columns.

✓

	Prevention Costs	Appraisal Costs	Internal Failure Costs	External Failure Costs
Production staff training costs				
Costs of customer complaints section				
Costs of re-inspection of reworked products				
Inspection of work in progress				
Testing of finished goods				
Loss of customer goodwill				
Customer compensation payments				

6

Chapter activities
Measuring performance

6.1   Complete the following table by selecting a valid method of calculation for each ratio.

Ratio Title		Calculation
(a)	Gross profit margin	**1** $\dfrac{\text{Sales}}{(\text{All Assets} - \text{Current Liabilities})}$
(b)	Debt to equity ratio	**2** $\dfrac{\text{Advertising Costs}}{\text{Sales}} \times 100$
(c)	Operating profit margin	**3** $\dfrac{\text{Current Assets}}{\text{Current Liabilities}}$
(d)	Return on capital employed	**4** $\dfrac{\text{Trade Receivables}}{\text{Credit Sales}} \times 365$
(e)	Advertising cost as a percentage of turnover	**5** $\dfrac{(\text{Total debt} + \text{Preference Share Capital})}{\text{Total Capital Employed}} \times 100$
(f)	Asset turnover	**6** $\dfrac{(\text{Current Assets} - \text{Inventory})}{\text{Current Liabilities}}$
(g)	Gearing ratio	**7** $\dfrac{\text{Gross Profit}}{\text{Sales}} \times 100$
(h)	Current ratio	**8** $\dfrac{\text{Profit before interest}}{\text{Capital Employed}} \times 100$
(i)	Receivables' payment period in days	**9** $\dfrac{\text{Profit before interest}}{\text{Sales}} \times 100$
(j)	Quick ratio	**10** $\dfrac{(\text{Total debt} + \text{Preference Share Capital})}{(\text{Ordinary Share Capital} + \text{Reserves})} \times 100$

6.2   A trading company has the following results:

Income Statement for the year ended 31 December				
	20-8		**20-7**	
	£	£	£	£
Sales		209,000		196,000
less cost of sales:				
Opening Inventory	24,000		25,000	
Purchases	155,000		150,000	
Closing Inventory	22,000		24,000	
		157,000		151,000
Gross Profit		52,000		45,000
Depreciation	9,000		9,000	
Sundry Expenses	14,000		11,000	
		23,000		20,000
Operating Profit		29,000		25,000
Interest		2,000		2,000
Net Profit		27,000		23,000
Taxation		10,000		10,000
Net Profit after taxation		17,000		13,000
Ordinary Dividends	6,000		5,000	
Preference Dividends	2,000		2,000	
		8,000		7,000
Retained Profit		9,000		6,000

Statement of Financial Position	As at 31/12/20-8	As at 31/12/20-7
	£	£
Non-current Assets	130,000	139,000
Current Assets:		
Inventory	22,000	24,000
Trade Receivables	40,000	36,000
Bank	12,000	5,000
	74,000	65,000
Current Liabilities:		
Trade Payables	46,000	45,000
Short term loans	0	20,000
Net Current Assets	28,000	0
Total Assets less Current Liabilities	158,000	139,000
Non-current Liabilities:		
5% secured loan stock	40,000	40,000
	118,000	99,000
Ordinary Share Capital (50p shares)	35,000	35,000
8% Preference Shares (£1 shares)	25,000	25,000
Share Premium Account	17,000	17,000
Revaluation Reserve	10,000	0
Retained Earnings	31,000	22,000
	118,000	99,000

Complete the following table to show the performance indicators listed for each year. Show the solutions to 2 decimal places, with the exception of those measured in days which should be rounded to the nearest day.

	20-8	20-7
Gross Profit %		
Return on Capital Employed %		
Operating Profit as % Sales		
Current Ratio		
Asset Turnover		
Quick Ratio		
Trade Receivables Days		
Trade Payables Days		
Gearing Ratio %		

6.3 The performance indicators shown in the following table have been calculated for a trading company. Match the comments on performance shown with the appropriate measure of performance.

Performance Indicator	20-8	20-7	Comments
Gross Profit %	24.88	22.96	The profit before interest as a percentage of turnover has increased in the later year
Return on Capital Employed %	18.35	17.99	There is less value of sales compared to total resources in the later year
Operating Profit as % Sales	13.88	12.76	The profit as a percentage of sales (after taking into account just the cost of sales) has improved from the first year to the second
Current Ratio	1.61	1.00	Credit customers are taking slightly longer on average to pay in the later year than they were in the previous year
Asset Turnover	1.32	1.41	There are more current assets compared to current liabilities in the later year
Quick Ratio	1.13	0.63	The operating profit as a percentage of total resources has increased from year to year
Trade Receivables Days	70	67	A smaller proportion of the capital employed is based on fixed interest capital in the later year
Trade Payables Days	108	158	After excluding inventory, there are more current assets compared to current liabilities in the later year
Gearing Ratio %	41.14	46.76	The company is paying its credit suppliers considerably more quickly in the later year

6.4 Utoxx Limited has developed a potion which claims to detoxify individuals. The product competes with those from several other companies. Meetox is a major competitor and market leader, with over half of the market. You have been given the following information about Utoxx and Meetox for the year just ended.

Income Statement	Utoxx	Meetox
	£000	£000
Turnover	12,000	50,000
Cost of production		
Direct (raw) materials	2,800	8,600
Direct labour	1,900	4,200
Fixed production overheads	1,500	9,000
Total cost of sales	6,200	21,800
Gross profit	**5,800**	**28,200**
Selling and distribution costs	1,200	2,000
Administration costs	950	2,500
Advertising costs	900	18,000
Net profit	2,750	5,700

Other information		Utoxx	Meetox
Number of units sold	*Units*	1,200,000	4,500,000
Net assets	*(£000)*	10,000	18,000

Calculate the performance indicators to complete the following table for Utoxx and Meetox:

Give answers to two decimal places.

	Utoxx	*Meetox*
Selling price per unit		
Material cost per unit		
Labour cost per unit		
Fixed production overheads per unit		
Gross profit margin		
Net profit margin		
Advertising cost as % of turnover		
Return on net assets		

7   Chapter activities
Measuring performance – further aspects

7.1   Control Limited makes a single product and uses standard costing.

Each unit has a standard labour time of 20 minutes. During November the budget was to produce 45,000 units.

In November 44,100 units were manufactured, and this took 15,200 labour hours.

Complete the following table by inserting the control ratios calculated as percentages to two decimal places.

Efficiency Ratio	
Activity Ratio (or Production Volume Ratio)	
Capacity Ratio	

7.2   Your organisation needs to send a parcel to an address on the other side of the city. It should arrive as soon as possible, but by tomorrow at the latest. Three alternatives have been suggested:

■   Hire a taxi straight away to take the parcel. It will take about an hour and will cost £40.

■   Send the parcel with a national 'overnight' parcel delivery service. This guarantees delivery by 9am tomorrow. The cost is £15.

■   Give the parcel to John, who works in your office. He intends to visit his grandmother tomorrow or the next day, and she lives close to where the parcel needs to be delivered. Since he is going anyway, he won't charge to deliver the parcel.

By ticking the appropriate columns in the table, decide which alternative is the most economic, most efficient and most effective, from your organisation's point of view.

✓

	Economic	Efficient	Effective
Use a taxi			
Use national 'overnight' service			
Let John take it			

7.3   Complete the following table by selecting a valid method of calculation for each performance indicator

Performance Indicator	Calculation
(a) Labour efficiency (or efficiency ratio)	**1** $$\frac{(\text{Sales} - \text{Cost of Materials and Bought-in Services})}{\text{Number of Employees}}$$
(b) Labour capacity (or capacity ratio)	**2** $$\frac{\text{Standard Hours for Actual Production}}{\text{Budgeted Standard Hours}} \text{ x 100}$$
(c) Added value per employee	**3** $$\frac{\text{Unfulfilled Orders (in units)}}{\text{Annual Sales (in units)}} \text{ x 12}$$
(d) Average delay in completing an order in months	**4** Sales – Cost of Materials and Bought-in Services
(e) Activity (or production volume) ratio	**5** $$\frac{\text{Sales}}{\text{Labour Hours Worked}}$$
(f) Value added	**6** $$\frac{\text{Sales}}{\text{Units Sold}}$$
(g) Average sales price per hour of labour	**7** $$\frac{\text{Actual Hours Worked}}{\text{Budgeted Standard Hours}} \text{ x 100}$$
(h) Average sales price per unit	**8** $$\frac{\text{Standard Hours for Actual Production}}{\text{Actual Hours Worked}} \text{ x 100}$$

7.4 The four perspectives used by the balanced scorecard are:

■   Financial

■   Customer

■   Internal

■   Innovation and Learning

The following table shows what each perspective is concerned with and ratios that can be used to measure aspects of that perspective.

Complete the table by inserting the correct perspective in each row.

Perspective	What it is concerned with	Typical ratios that can be used
	Technical excellence and quality issues	Added Value, Cost of Quality, Reject Rates, Sales returns (due to quality issues) as a % of net sales.
	Customer satisfaction and loyalty	Delivery times (or order backlogs), Repeat orders from customers, Sales returns as a % of net sales.
	Improvement of existing products or services, and development of new products or services	R & D Expenditure (or as %), Revenue from new products (or as %).
	Satisfying the shareholders, primarily by generating profits	Gross Profit %, Operating Profit %, ROCE, Added Value.

8 Chapter activities
Scenario planning

8.1 Tinnitt Limited, a canned food manufacturer, currently makes two products in its factory. The first is baked beans, and the second is garden peas. Both are sold in tins.

The following budgeted operating statement relates to the next year, and assumes that both products will be manufactured in-house. It is based on making and selling 2,000,000 units of baked beans, and 1,000,000 units of garden peas.

	£'000	£'000	£'000
	Beans	**Peas**	**Total**
Sales	400	220	620
Variable costs of production	120	80	200
Direct fixed costs of production	80	70	150
Shared fixed costs of production	100	50	150
Gross profit	100	20	120
Administration costs			40
Selling and distribution costs			30
Operating profit			50

Consideration is being given to an option to buy in ready made tinned peas at £0.14 per unit. This would save both the variable costs of production and the direct fixed costs of production of that product. Shared fixed costs of production would remain the same in total. The number of units of tinned peas sold would be unchanged.

If the decision were made to buy in the tinned peas, then the released manufacturing space could be used to increase the manufacture and sales of baked beans to 2,500,000 units, with some spare capacity remaining. The direct fixed costs of baked bean production would be unchanged by this. To cope with the increased total volume of sales, the selling and distribution costs would increase by £5,000, but administration costs would remain unchanged.

Complete the table on the following page to show a budgeted operating statement based on the position if the decision were made to buy in tinned peas and increase production of baked beans.

	Baked Beans	Garden Peas	Total
Volume (units)	2,500,000	1,000,000	
	£'000	£'000	£'000
Sales			
Variable costs of production / purchase			
Direct fixed costs of production			
Previously shared fixed costs of production			
Gross profit			
Administration costs			
Selling and distribution costs			
Operating profit			

8.2 Beta Limited manufactures toothpaste and is considering launching an improved version to replace the current product. It will be sold in smaller packs since it will be most effective when less quantity is used.

- Current sales volume is 2.0 million units per annum and this is not expected to change.

- Current fixed production costs are £0.6 million.

- Current labour cost per unit is £1.05 which is completely variable.

- Current material cost per unit is £1.45 and is completely variable.

- Assume stock levels are kept at zero.

- Variable material cost of the new product will be £0.30 less per unit than the current toothpaste.

- Selling price will be increased from £5.50 to £6.00.

- Fixed selling and distribution costs will reduce from £600,000 to £500,000.

- Additional investment in assets will be £8 million which will be depreciated at £800,000 per annum.

- All other costs will remain the same.

(a) Calculate the total annual increase in profit by completing the table below.

	Units	Price/cost	Total £
Additional revenue			
Savings on materials			
Reduction in selling and distribution costs			
Additional depreciation			
Additional annual profit			

(b) Based on the new product, calculate the performance measures shown in the following table to help understand any additional risk.

Return on additional investment (%)	
Total fixed costs	
Contribution per unit	
Break even sales volume in units	
Margin of safety (%)	

8.3 The table below shows the current situation for a company that buys and sells a single product. Current sales are 2,500 units per month, based on a selling price of £15.

Inventory is valued at variable cost and is equal to 3 months' sales. Customers take 2.5 months to pay. Payables relate to variable costs and are paid in 2 months.

A suggestion has been made to reduce the selling price by 20% to £12, which it is thought will result in an increased sales volume of 40%.

Complete the table based on the proposal, assuming that net current asset periods remain the same.

	Current Position	Proposed Position
Monthly Income Statement	£	£
Sales	37,500	
Variable Costs	25,000	
Fixed Costs	5,000	
Operating Profit	7,500	
Net Current Assets		
Inventory	75,000	
Receivables	93,750	
Less Payables	(50,000)	
Total Net Current Assets (exc cash)	118,750	

8.4 Chippum Limited makes frozen potato chips from raw potatoes. The potatoes are first machine washed, and then put through a peeling and slicing machine where the chips are cut to shape. At this stage a quality check is carried out by staff who manually pick out from the conveyor system and discard any chips that have blemishes. The chips are then cooked, frozen and bagged ready for sale.

The manager has been investigating the purchase of automated quality control line equipment that would eliminate the need for the majority of employees. The purchase and installation of the equipment would cost £600,000, and would be depreciated at £120,000 per year.

The following income statement is based on the next year's operation, assuming the current working practices, and production of 1 million packs of chips.

	£'000
Sales	1,200
less:	
Variable material cost	300
Variable labour cost	250
Contribution	650
less:	
Fixed production costs	100
Fixed administration costs	300
Operating profit	250

The net operating assets of the business are currently £1,600,000.

If the automated quality control line is installed:

■   labour costs will reduce to £90,000 per year, regardless of the production level

■   fixed production costs will increase by £20,000 per year, in addition to the depreciation expense

■   other costs will be unchanged

The company's cost of capital is 5%, and discount factors over the five year life of the project are as follows:

Year	Discount factor 5%	Year	Discount factor 5%
0	1.00	3	0.864
1	0.952	4	0.823
2	0.907	5	0.784

The automated line will be paid for immediately and have no value at the end of the five year project. Assume that sales and costs remain at the same level for each of the five years, and occur at the end of each year.

Using the following table, calculate the net present value of the mechanisation project.

Year	Cash Outflow £'000	Cash Savings £'000	Discount Factor	Present Value £'000
0				
1				
2				
3				
4				
5				
	Net Present Value			

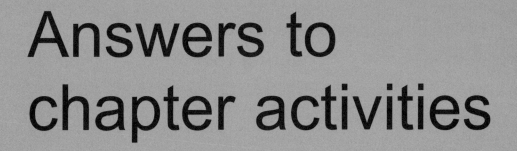

Answers to chapter activities

Chapter activities – answers
Management accounting techniques

1.1   The trend in prices is an increase of £0.30 per month.

1.2   (c)   120   *(Cost per kilo £18.00 compared with £15.00)*

1.3   (a)   The cost index in April was 135 and the increase from January to April is 8.0%

1.4

Feature	Marginal Costing	Absorption Costing
Can be used to set a minimum selling price	✓	
Complies with standard IAS 2 for inventory valuation		✓
Can be used for planning and control but is of limited use for decision making		✓
Can be used in conjunction with break-even analysis	✓	
Can be used in conjunction with 'full cost plus' pricing		✓
Is often used in conjunction with discounted cash flow decision making techniques	✓	

1.5   (a)

Year	Detail	Cash Flow £	Discount Factor	Present Value £
0	Purchase and Installation	(8,000)	1.000	(8,000)
1	Savings and increased house sale proceeds	200	0.909	182
2		200	0.826	165
3		200	0.751	150
4		200	0.683	137
5		5,200	0.621	3,229
Net Present Value				(4,137)

   (b)   The net present value of the scheme is **negative** so from a financial point of view the scheme is **not worthwhile**.

1.6 The difference in total cost of £152,000 - £100,000 = £52,000 is due to the variable costs for 18,000 − 10,000 = 8,000 units.

Variable costs per unit are therefore

   £52,000 / 8,000   = £6.50 per unit.

Fixed costs account for the difference between the variable costs and the total costs.

At 10,000 units:

Total costs	£100,000
Variable costs (10,000 x £6.50)	£ 65,000
Therefore fixed costs are	£ 35,000

The same answer could be obtained using the 18,000 unit costs.

1.7 The difference in total cost of £606,000 - £500,000 = £106,000 is due to

■　　the step in fixed costs of £40,000

■　　the variable costs for 28,000 − 22,000 = 6,000 units.

Variable costs per unit are therefore

(£106,000 - £40,000) / 6,000= £11.00 per unit.

Fixed costs account for the difference between the variable costs and the total costs.

At 22,000 units:

Total costs	£500,000
Variable costs (22,000 x £11)	£242,000
Therefore stepped fixed costs are	£258,000

At 28,000 units:

Total costs	£606,000
Variable costs (28,000 x £11)	£308,000
Therefore stepped fixed costs are	£298,000

This also agrees with the step in the fixed cost of £40,000.

2

Chapter activities – answers
Standard costing – direct costs

2.1 (d) £600 Favourable

2.2 (b) £1,300 Adverse

2.3 (a) £87,500

2.4

Variance	£	A/F
Direct material (paint) price variance	130	F
Direct material (sheet steel) usage variance	750	A
Direct labour rate variance	2,050	A
Direct labour efficiency variance	6,000	F

Variance Workings:

Paint price:	*(650 litres x £5) – £3,120*	*= £130 F*
Steel usage:	*((11,500 x 3) – 35,000) x £1.50*	*= £750 A*
Labour rate:	*(4,100 x £12) – £51,250)*	*= £2,050 A*
Labour efficiency:	*((11,500 x 0.4) – 4,100) x £12*	*= £6,000 F*

2.5 **(a)** The standard material cost per kg is **£1.40**

  (b) The standard quantity of material to make one unit is **0.5kg**

  (c) The standard cost of the materials to make one unit is **£0.70**

Workings:

(a) (£15,400 + £700) / 11,500 kg = £1.40 per kg

(b) (£700 / £1.40 = 500 kg) + 11,500 kg = 12,000 kg

   12,000 kg / 24,000 units = 0.5 kg per unit

(c) £1.40 x 0.5kg per unit = £0.70

2.6 The standard time to make 2,000 units is **400** hours.

   Working: 2,000 units x 12/60 hours

  The standard labour rate is **£10** per hour.

   Working: £450 = (445 – 400) hours x Standard rate
   Therefore Standard rate = £450 / 45 hours

2.7   The standard hourly rate is **£11.00** per hour.

> *Working: Standard cost of 5,500 hours is £59,400 + £1,100 = £60,500*
>
> *Standard hourly rate is £60,500 / 5,500 hours*

2.8

Budgeted / Standard cost of materials for actual production			97,500
Variances	**Favourable**	**Adverse**	
Direct material price	1,560		
Direct material usage		3,900	
Total variance		2,340	+2,340
Actual cost of materials for actual production			99,840

2.9

Budgeted / Standard cost of labour for actual production			3,750.00
Variances	**Favourable**	**Adverse**	
Direct labour rate		107.50	
Direct labour efficiency		87.50	
Total variance		195.00	+195.00
Actual cost of labour for actual production			3,945.00

3

Chapter activities – answers
Standard costing – fixed overheads

3.1

1 unit of Zed	Quantity	Cost per unit £	Total cost £
Material	12 kg	8.50	102.00
Labour	0.6 hour	15.00	9.00
Fixed costs	1 unit	80.00	80.00
Total			191.00

3.2   The fixed overhead volume variance is £100,000 **adverse**.

The fixed overhead expenditure variance is £20,000 **favourable.**

3.3   The fixed overhead efficiency variance is £4,800 **adverse**.

The fixed overhead capacity variance is £11,200 **adverse.**

3.4

	Variance £	A / F	Variance £	A / F
Expenditure Variance			2,000	F
Capacity Variance	1,500	A		
Efficiency Variance	4,500	A		
Volume Variance			6,000	A
Total Fixed Overhead Variances			4,000	A

3.5   (a) and (c) are false; the others are true.

3.6

Budgeted / Standard fixed cost for actual production			437,500
Variances	**Favourable**	**Adverse**	
Fixed overhead expenditure	10,500		
Fixed overhead volume	7,500		
Total variance	18,000		-18,000
Actual fixed cost for actual production			419,500

4

Chapter activities – answers
Standard costing – further analysis

4.1

Budgeted cost for actual production			39,165
Variances:	Favourable	Adverse	
Direct materials (liquid cleaner) price	975		
Direct materials (liquid cleaner) usage		125	
Direct materials (bottles) price	96		
Direct materials (bottles) usage		60	
Direct labour rate	170		
Direct labour efficiency		330	
Fixed overhead expenditure		500	
Fixed overhead volume	350		
Total variances	1,591	1,015	-576
Actual cost of actual production			38,589

4.2

Budgeted cost for actual production			81,120
Variances:	Favourable	Adverse	
Direct materials price	80		
Direct materials usage		80	
Direct labour rate		600	
Direct labour efficiency		400	
Fixed overhead expenditure		2,300	
Fixed overhead capacity	4,500		
Fixed overhead efficiency		2,000	
Total variances	4,580	5,380	+ 800
Actual cost of actual production			81,920

4.2   (continued)

Variance workings:

DMPV	(800 x £4) - £3,120	= £80 F
DMUV	[(3 litres x 260) – 800 litres] x £4	= £80 A
DLRV	(1,340 hrs x £10) - £14,000	= £600 A
DLEV	[(5 hrs x 260) – 1,340 hrs] x £10	= £400 A
FO Exp	£62,500 - £64,800	= £2,300 A
FO Cap	(1,340 x £50) – (1,250 x £50)	= £4,500 F
FO Eff	(1,300 x £50) – (1,340 x £50)	= £2,000 A

4.3

Direct Material Usage Variance			Part of variance caused by change in product specification			Part of variance caused by unknown factors		
	£	A / F		£	A / F		£	A / F
	2,400	F		9,000	F		6,600	A

4.4

email	
To:	Production Director
From:	Accounting Technician
Date:	xx
Subject:	Reasons for Variances

The following sets out some possible reasons for the adverse variances that occurred based on the September operations.

The direct material price variance relates to the buying price of raw potatoes. The recent UK weather created a poor potato harvest, and the subsequent shortage of potatoes led to a price increase. This price increase would have been across the whole UK market.

The direct material usage variance relates to the additional cost incurred due to using more raw potatoes than expected to make the average bag of frozen chips. This appears to be due to the poor quality of potatoes, which meant that more partly processed output had to be rejected.

The adverse direct labour rate variance may be caused by the use of overtime rates to pay for the additional time required by the quality control operatives. The overtime rate was paid to satisfy the need to spend more time discarding the blemished chips that occurred due to the quality of the potatoes.

The direct labour efficiency variance is also related to the work of the labour-intensive quality control function. Since there were so many blemished chips to be removed, the conveyor had to be slowed down, and this increased the labour time needed to check the output.

The fixed overhead expenditure variance relates to the additional fixed overheads incurred in September. One such cost was incurred when the conveyor broke down and a contractor was utilised to supply and fit replacement parts.

The fixed overhead volume variance is caused by spreading the fixed overheads over a smaller amount of output than was budgeted. It seems likely that in September the output was lower than budgeted due to the greater proportion of the input that was rejected in the form of blemished chips, together with the linked issue of the slow running of the conveyor.

Overall the adverse variances mean that the actual cost of the September production was £30,000 more than the standard cost of the same production level.

4.5

Budgeted / Standard variable cost for actual production			883,350
Budgeted fixed costs			200,000
Variances	Favourable	Adverse	
Direct materials (drink) price		29,300	
Direct materials (drink) usage		1,050	
Direct materials (cans) price		0	
Direct materials (cans) usage		200	
Direct labour rate	300		
Direct labour efficiency	300		
Fixed overhead expenditure		3,500	
Total variance		33,450	+33,450
Actual cost of actual production			1,116,800

Workings:

Budgeted variable cost for actual production:

(£630,000 + £240,000 + £36,000) x 5,850,000 / 6,000,000 = £883,350

Direct materials (drink) price variance

(2,930,000 litres x £0.21*) - £644,600 = £29,300 A

　　　*£630,000 / 3,000 litres

Direct materials (drink) usage variance

((5,850,000 units x 0.5*) – 2,930,000) x £0.21 = £1,050 A

　　　*500 ml = 0.5 litre

Direct materials (cans) price variance

(5,855,000 units x £0.04) - £234,200 = £0

Direct materials (cans) usage variance

(5,850,000 – 5,855,000) x £0.04 = £200 A

Direct labour rate variance

(2,900 x £12*) - £34,500 = £300 F

　　　*£36,000 / 3,000 hours

Direct labour efficiency variance

((5,850,000 units x 0.0005 hours per unit*) – 2,900 hours) x £12 = £300 F

　　　*3,000 hours / 6,000,000 units

Fixed overhead expenditure variance

£200,000 - £203,500 = £3,500 A

5 Chapter activities – answers
Measuring quality

5.1

Maximum production cost per unit	£5.25
Build up of maximum production cost per unit:	
Materials	£1.85 (balancing figure)
Labour	£1.40
Overheads	£2.00
Maximum cost per kilo for material T	£3.70

5.2 **(a)**

Year	0	1	2	3	4
Cash flow	15,000	800	800	800	(3,200)
Discount factor	1.00	0.952	0.907	0.864	0.823
Present value	15,000	762	726	691	(2,634)
Net present cost	14,545				

(b)

Year	0	1	2	3	4
Lease costs	4,100	4,100	4,100	4,100	0
Discount factor	1.00	0.952	0.907	0.864	0.823
Present value	4,100	3,903	3,719	3,542	0
Net present cost	15,264				

(c) Based on the calculations it is best to **purchase** each van, which saves a net present amount of £719.

5.3   **(a)**

	£
Sales price per unit	40.00
Profit margin	18.00
Total costs	22.00
Fixed cost per unit	12.00
Labour cost per unit	6.00
Maximum material cost per unit	4.00
Target cost per kilogram	20.00

(b)   The trade price quoted on the supplier's price list is £25 per kilogram. The purchasing manager has negotiated a discount of 15%. The discount should be **rejected** because the £25 reduces to **£21.25** which is **above** the Target cost.

(c)   The minimum percentage discount needed to achieve the Target cost is 20%

5.4

	Prevention Costs	Appraisal Costs	Internal Failure Costs	External Failure Costs
Production staff training costs	✓			
Costs of customer complaints section				✓
Costs of re-inspection of reworked products			✓	
Inspection of work in progress		✓		
Testing of finished goods		✓		
Loss of customer goodwill				✓
Customer compensation payments				✓

6 Chapter activities – answers
Measuring performance

6.1 (a) 7

(b) 10

(c) 9

(d) 8

(e) 2

(f) 1

(g) 5

(h) 3

(i) 4

(j) 6

6.2

	20-8	*20-7*
Gross Profit %	24.88	22.96
Return on Capital Employed %	18.35	17.99
Operating Profit as % Sales	13.88	12.76
Current Ratio	1.61	1.00
Asset Turnover	1.32	1.41
Quick Ratio	1.13	0.63
Trade Receivables Days	70	67
Trade Payables Days	108	110
Gearing Ratio %	41.14	53.46

6.3

Performance Indicator	20-8	20-7	Comments
Gross Profit %	24.88	22.96	The profit as a percentage of sales (after taking into account just the cost of sales) has improved from the first year to the second
Return on Capital Employed %	18.35	17.99	The operating profit as a percentage of total resources has increased from year to year
Operating Profit as % Sales	13.88	12.76	The profit before interest as a percentage of turnover has increased in the later year
Current Ratio	1.61	1.00	There are more current assets compared to current liabilities in the later year
Asset Turnover	1.32	1.41	There is less value of sales compared to total resources in the later year
Quick Ratio	1.13	0.63	After excluding inventory, there are more current assets compared to current liabilities in the later year
Trade Receivables Days	70	67	Credit customers are taking slightly longer on average to pay in the later year than they were in the previous year
Trade Payables Days	108	158	The company is paying its credit suppliers considerably more quickly in the later year
Gearing Ratio %	41.14	46.76	A smaller proportion of the capital employed is based on fixed interest capital in the later year

6.4

	Utoxx	Meetox
Selling price per unit	£10.00	£11.11
Material cost per unit	£2.33	£1.91
Labour cost per unit	£1.58	£0.93
Fixed production overheads per unit	£1.25	£2.00
Gross profit margin	48.33%	56.40%
Net profit margin	22.92%	11.40%
Advertising cost as % of turnover	7.50%	36.00%
Return on net assets	27.50%	31.67%

7

Chapter activities – answers
Measuring performance – further aspects

7.1

Efficiency Ratio	96.71%
Activity Ratio (or Production Volume Ratio)	98.00%
Capacity Ratio	101.33%

7.2

	Economic	*Efficient*	*Effective*
Use a taxi			✓
Use national 'overnight' service		✓	
Let John take it	✓		

7.3   (a)   8

        (b)   7

        (c)   1

        (d)   3

        (e)   2

        (f)   4

        (g)   5

        (h)   6

7.4

Perspective	What it is concerned with	Typical ratios that can be used
Internal	Technical excellence and quality issues	Added Value, Cost of Quality, Reject Rates, Sales returns (due to quality issues) as a % of net sales.
Customer	Customer satisfaction and loyalty	Delivery times (or order backlogs), Repeat orders from customers, Sales returns as a % of net sales.
Innovation and Learning	Improvement of existing products or services, and development of new products or services	R & D Expenditure (or as %), Revenue from new products (or as %).
Financial	Satisfying the shareholders, primarily by generating profits	Gross Profit %, Operating Profit %, ROCE, Added Value.

8

Chapter activities – answers
Scenario planning

8.1

	Baked Beans	Garden Peas	Total
Volume (units)	2,500,000	1,000,000	
	£'000	£'000	£'000
Sales	500	220	720
Variable costs of production / purchase	150	140	290
Direct fixed costs of production	80	0	80
Previously shared fixed costs of production	150	0	150
Gross profit	120	80	200
Administration costs			40
Selling and distribution costs			35
Operating profit			125

8.2   (a)

	Units	Price/cost £	Total £
Additional revenue	2,000,000	0.50	1,000,000
Savings on materials	2,000,000	0.30	600,000
Reduction in selling and distribution costs			100,000
Additional depreciation			(800,000)
Additional annual profit			900,000

(b)

Return on additional investment (%)	11.25%
Total fixed costs	£1,900,000
Contribution per unit	£3.80
Break even sales volume in units	500,000
Margin of safety (%)	75%

8.3

	Current Position	Proposed Position
Monthly Income Statement	£	£
Sales	37,500	42,000
Variable Costs	25,000	35,000
Fixed Costs	5,000	5,000
Operating Profit	7,500	2,000
Net Current Assets		
Inventory	75,000	105,000
Receivables	93,750	105,000
Less Payables	(50,000)	(70,000)
Total Net Current Assets (exc cash)	118,750	140,000

8.4

Year	Cash Outflow	Cash Savings	Discount Factor	Present Value
	£'000	£'000		£'000
0	600,000		1.000	(600,000)
1		140,000	0.952	133,280
2		140,000	0.907	126,980
3		140,000	0.864	120,960
4		140,000	0.823	115,220
5		140,000	0.784	109,760
	Net Present Value			6,200

Cash savings:

Labour savings	£160,000
Less increased production costs	£ 20,000
	£140,000

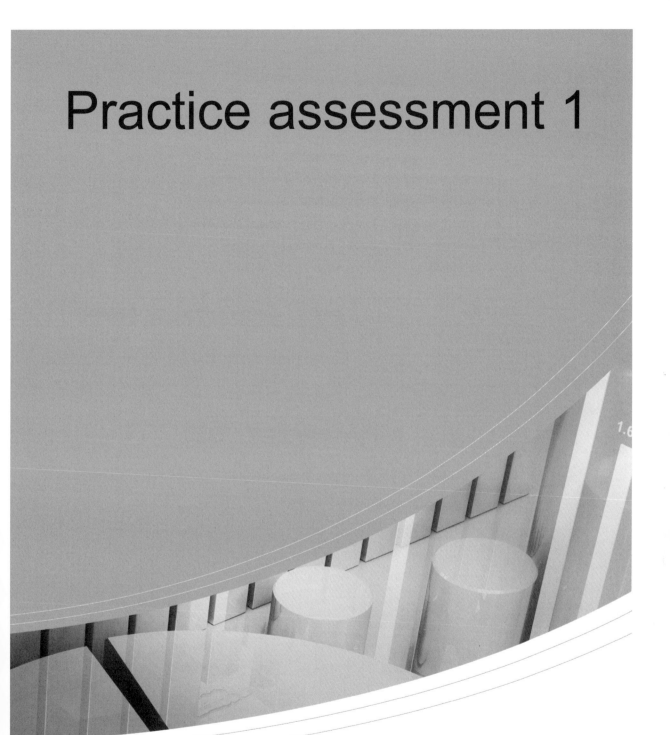

Practice assessment 1

Section 1

Task 1.1

(a) The following information has been calculated for the production of 1 unit of Exe:

■ Each unit will require 1.3 kilograms of material at a cost of £4.50 per kilogram

■ Each unit will require 0.2 hours of labour at a total cost of £3.60

■ Fixed overheads total £50,000 and the estimated output will be 25,000 units of Zed

■ Fixed overheads are absorbed on a labour hour basis

Complete the standard cost card below.

1 unit of Exe	Quantity	Cost per unit £	Total cost £
Material	1.3	~~54.50~~	5-85
Labour	.2	18.00	3.60
Fixed costs	.2	2.00	2.00
Total			11.45

(b) A manufacturer uses 30,000 kg of material to make 150,000 units. The standard quantity of material for each unit is:

$$0.2 \text{ kg} = \frac{30000}{150,000}$$

1.1. WORKINGS

Mat   1.3 kg @ £4.50 = £5.85

Lat   .2 hr @ £18 ,   3-60

.2 hr @ £10 /hr

$$\frac{2.00}{11.45}$$

25000 units x .2

= 5000 hrs

Total o/H 50000

5000

£10 /hr

Task 1.2

1. A company purchases 18,000 kilograms of material at a cost of £91,080. The standard cost per kilogram is £5.10. The total material price variance is:

		✓
(a)	£720 Favourable	✓
(b)	£0.04 Favourable	
(c)	£720 Adverse	
(d)	£0.04 Adverse	

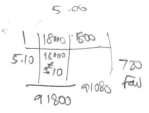

2. A company used 11,000 kilograms of material at a cost of £47,300. The production was 1,200 units, for which the standard usage is 10,800 kilograms of material at a total standard cost of £43,200. The material usage variance is:

		✓
(a)	200 kg Adverse	✓
(b)	£3,300 Adverse	
(c)	£800 Adverse	✓
(d)	£860 Adverse	

11000 kg @ 47300
1200 units → 10800 kg = £32
= 4

St 10800 kg
Act 11000 kg
200 kg × 4 = 800 Adverse

3. A company expects to produce 10,000 units of Y using 5,000 labour hours. The standard cost of labour is £20 per hour. If the actual output is 12,500 units, what is the standard labour cost for this output?

		✓
(a)	£500,000	
(b)	£250,000	
(c)	£125,000	✓
(d)	£50,000	

10000 U = 5000 hrs

1 hr   5000 / 10000 = ½ hr = £10

12500 × 10

4. A company used 11,000 kilograms of material at a cost of £47,300. The production was 1,200 units, for which the standard usage is 10,800 kilograms of material at a total standard cost of £43,200. The material price variance is:

		✓
(a)	£800 Adverse	
(b)	£3,300 Adverse	✓
(c)	£3,240 Adverse	
(d)	£860 Adverse	

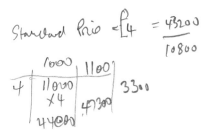

Task 1.3

Variance 400000
Act 415000 = 1500

4000
42000
2000 Fav = 2000 × 10
42000 × 10 = 420000

(a) You have been given the following information:

- Budgeted overheads are £400,000
- Budgeted output is 40,000 units
- Actual output is 42,000 units
- Actual overheads are £415,000

Absorption Cost - Budgeted OH 400000
Budget per unit 40000
£10 per unit

The fixed overhead volume variance is £ 20000 ~~adverse~~ / **favourable.**

budgeted 400000
actual 415000

The fixed overhead expenditure variance is £ 15000 **adverse** / ~~favourable~~.

(b) You have been given the following information:

- Budgeted overheads are £90,000
- Budgeted output is 15,000 units and 5,000 labour hours
- Actual output is 14,400 units and 4,950 actual labour hours
- Actual overheads are £93,000

90000 / 15000 = 6

6600

Var
3600
900   2700

The fixed overhead efficiency variance is £ 2700 **adverse** / ~~favourable~~.

The fixed overhead capacity variance is £ 900 ~~adverse~~ / **favourable.**

Capacity = Budgt - Actual h
variance
(5000 - 4950) × 18
900 Adverse

Eff = St for actual ≠ Actual h/Std
= 1/3 h × 14400 - 4950) 18
= 4800 - 4950 × 18
= 2700 Adverse

① Absop Rate Per unit 90000/15000 = £6 per unit

② Absorb rate per hrs 90000/5000 = £18 per hr

Exp Variance = Bud Exp - Act Exp
= 90000 - 93000
= 3000 Adv

Volume (Budget units - Actual units) unit rate
= 15000 - 14400
= 600 × 6 = 3600

[handwritten: 50 000 → 20000 = ·4]
[handwritten: 20000 — 60000]
[handwritten: 1 KG = ⅗]
[handwritten: STANDARD COST CARD]
[handwritten: Instant coffee | Usage | Price | Cost]
[handwritten: ·4 KG | £3 KG | 1·2 unit]

Task 1.4

A company packs instant coffee into jars.

The following budgetary control report has been provided:

[handwritten: Cost ·04]
[handwritten: Jar ·04]
[handwritten: 200 → 3600]
[handwritten: 1 = 18]
[handwritten: 50000 = 200]
[handwritten: = ·004 × 18   0.072]

	Budget		Actual	
Production (jars)		50,000		51,500
Instant coffee	20,000 kg	£60,000	20,650 kg	£62,260
Glass jars	50,000 units	£2,000	51,700 units	£2,050
Direct labour	200 hours	£3,600	220 hours	£3,850
Fixed overheads		£10,000		£10,150
Total cost		£75,600		£78,310

[handwritten alongside: £3 ; 1.2 ; 200/3600=18 ; ·004 ; 200/3600=18]

The following variances have been accurately calculated, although for some it is not known whether they are adverse or favourable:

Fixed overhead expenditure	£150 A
Direct materials (instant coffee) price	£310
Direct materials (glass jars) price	£18 F
Direct materials (instant coffee) usage	£150 A
Direct materials (glass jars) usage	£8
Direct labour rate	£110 F
Direct labour efficiency	£252
Fixed overhead volume	£300

[handwritten: SP × AQB − AP × AGB]
[handwritten: 3 × 20650 → 62260   60000]
[handwritten: = 310 A   20000]
[handwritten: STANDARD COST CARD Usage Instant coffee]
[handwritten: 200 hr → 10000 = £50 ph]
[handwritten: 50 × ·004 = £ 0·20]

Complete the following operating statement, including the budgeted cost for the 51,500 units of production and the variances. Make sure that the total agrees with the actual cost of production.

[handwritten: Total cost]
[handwritten: Material variance]
[handwritten: = 6 × 51500 = 62260   = Standard cost   =   60000/50000 = k]
[handwritten: 5 460 mat   (460) A]
[handwritten: 310 / 150   PRICE   USAGE]
[handwritten: usage variance]
[handwritten: Standard usage Actual output − Act usage   50000 − 20000 × Standard price = ·4]
[handwritten: (·4 × 51500 − 20650) × 3   = 150 Adverse]

1.2
04
1.512 × 5½500
072
.20
1.512

Budgeted cost for actual production			77868
Variances:	Favourable	Adverse	
Direct materials (instant coffee) price		310	
Direct materials (instant coffee) usage		150	
Direct materials (glass jars) price	18		
Direct materials (glass jars) usage		8	
Direct labour rate	110		
Direct labour efficiency		252	
Fixed overhead expenditure		150	
Fixed overhead volume	300		
Total variances	428	870	442
Actual cost of actual production			78310

Standard Cost Card   Instant Coffee   usage .4kg   price £3/kg   Cost 1.2 units
Jar   1 Jr   0.04   .04

0.004w/£18 0.072
1.512 × 51500

Task 1.5

1. The table below contains the last three months' cost per kilogram for product Beta.

Act P - Seasonal Variation

January	February	March
Actual price was £35.60	Actual price was £30.10	Actual price was £29.00
Seasonal variation was +£5.20	Seasonal variation was -£0.90	Seasonal variation was -£2.60

35. 60
- 5.2
------
30. 4

30.1
+ 90

31

29.00
2.60

31-6

The trend in prices is an **increase/decrease** of £ ⬚ .60 per month.

2. A company has provided the following information:

	January	February	March
Total cost	£120,000	£143,925	£143,100
Total quantity purchased	8,000 kg	9,500 kg	9,000 kg

15   1515   15.9

The cost index for March based upon January being the base period of 100 is:

	✓
(a) 119	
(b) 113	
(c) 143	
(d) 106	✓

15.9
---- = 106
15

3. The cost per unit of a product has decreased from £250 in January to £244 in April. The cost per unit was £200 when the index was rebased to 100.

		✓
(a)	The cost index in April was 125 and the decrease from January to April is 6.0%	
(b)	The cost index in April was 122 and the decrease from January to April is 2.4%	✓
(c)	The cost index in April is 122 and the decrease from January to April is 2.5%	
(d)	The cost index in April is 244 and the decrease from January to April is 2.4%	

J   250
A   244
B
100 = £200
Base

244 x100 = 122
200

6 x100 = 2.4
250

Task 1.6

Frooyo manufactures fruit yoghurts, using mechanised production lines. The production line for strawberry yoghurt is set to mix 400 grams of yoghurt with 100 grams of strawberries into each 500 gram pot. This minimum quantity of strawberries in each pot is displayed on the pot for consumers to see.

The monthly report on the strawberry yoghurt production line in September noted the following variances.

Material Variances	Favourable £	Adverse £
Direct material (yoghurt) price		£500
Direct material (yoghurt) usage	£20,000	
Direct material (strawberries) price		£30,000
Direct material (strawberries) usage		£50,000

During September, 2 million pots of strawberry yoghurt were produced. The standard price of yoghurt is 20p per kg, and the standard price of strawberries is 50p per kg.

You have discovered the following information about the September production of strawberry yoghurt.

- The strawberries are sourced in the UK. Due to poor UK weather the price rose by 10p per kilo above standard.

- Each yoghurt pot is automatically weighed to check that it contains a full 500 grams.

- The production equipment malfunctioned and inserted more strawberries and less yoghurt into each pot than it was supposed to. The total weight of each pot remained accurate.

- The equipment malfunction was not detected until after the month end.

- Variances of more than £1,000 are considered significant.

Using the above information, prepare a report for the Production Director. The report should:

- Explain and provide reasons for each significant material variance, and

- Suggest strategies that may minimise similar variances in future.

email

to: Production Director

from: Accounting technician

date: xx/xx/xxxx

subject: Report on September production of strawberry yoghurt

Price Variances

- Explanation and reasons

- Future strategies

Quality control of equipment

Usage Variances

- Explanation and reasons

Maintained regularly - due to Malfunction

- Future strategies

Section 2

Task 2.1

Cosy Hotels Limited operates a number of small hotels. One of its competitors is Lush Hotels. You have been given the following information about Cosy Hotels and Lush Hotels for the year just ended.

Income Statement	Cosy	Lush
	£	£
Turnover	1,312,500	1,680,000
Variable costs		
Food	350,000	432,000
Laundry	87,500	120,000
Cleaning	262,500	288,000
Total variable costs	700,000	840,000
Contribution	**612,500**	**840,000**
Selling and marketing costs	300,000	350,000
Administration costs	155,000	163,000
Financial costs	85,000	118,000
Net profit	**72,500**	**209,000**

Other information	Cosy	Lush
Number of room-nights occupied	17,500	24,000
Number of room-nights available	35,000	30,000

Calculate the performance indicators to complete the following table for Cosy Hotels and Lush Hotels:

Give answers to two decimal places.

cosy   lush

Turnover / occupied $\frac{1312500}{17500} = 75$

occ Rate $\frac{17500}{35000} = 50\%$

	Cosy	Lush
Selling price per room-night	75	70
Occupancy rate (%)	50%	80%
Variable costs per room-night	£40	£35
Contribution per room-night	£35	£35
Contribution / sales ratio (%)	46.67%	50%
Net profit margin	5.52%	12.44%
Selling and marketing cost as % of turnover	22.86%	20.83%

612500 / 17500

700000 / 17500

618600 x100 / 1312500

Net P / Sales

Sell.mkt 300000
Turn 1312500

Task 2.2

Gamma Limited manufactures a food paste that is currently sold in jars and is considering launching a more concentrated version to replace the current product. It will be sold in small tubes.

■ Current sales volume is 3.0 million units per annum and this is not expected to change.

■ Current fixed production costs are £0.7 million.   *7 00000*

■ Current labour cost per unit is £0.55 which is completely variable.   *1650600*

■ Current material cost per unit is £0.95 and is completely variable.   *2850000*

■ Assume stock levels are kept at zero.

■ Variable material cost of the new product will be £0.15 less per unit than the current food product.

■ Selling price will be increased from £2.60 to £2.70.

■ Fixed selling and distribution costs will reduce from £400,000 to £250,000.

■ Additional investment in assets will be £4 million which will be depreciated at £400,000 per annum.

■ All other costs will remain the same.

(a) Calculate the total annual increase in profit by completing the table below.

	Units	Price/cost £	Total £
Additional revenue *.3m×10p*	*3 000 000*	*.10*	*300000*
Savings on materials	*300000*	*.15*	*450 00*
Reduction in selling and distribution costs			*150000*
Additional depreciation			*400000*
Additional annual profit			*500000*

(b)   Based on the new product, calculate the performance measures shown in the following table to help understand any additional risk.

Return on additional investment (%)	$\frac{500000}{4000000} \times 100$ 8 %
Total fixed costs	7000000 + 400000 + 2500000 per – 1350 000
Contribution per unit	SP – VC = 1.35
Break even sales volume in units	$\frac{1350000}{1.35}$ = 1000000
Margin of safety (%)	Sales – Break over $\div$ Sales ×100 66.67 %

will be

Current   2.6   2.70   3
    –   .55   – .55
    –   .95   – .80
         _____   _____
            1.10   1.35

Current Cont

Bredko   Fixed Cost
         ─────────────
         Cont. per unit

Task 2.3

Omega Limited is considering designing a new product, and will use target costing to arrive at the target cost of the product. You have been given the following information and asked to calculate the target cost for labour so that the production manager can calculate the labour time that should be allowed for manufacture.

- The price at which the product will be sold is £30
- The company has firm orders for 20,000 units at this price for the first year
- The fixed costs are £180,000 per year
- The labour rate is currently £15 per hour
- The required profit margin is 40% $30 \times 40\% = 12$
- The material requirement is 250 grams per unit
- The material cost is £16 per kg

(a) Calculate the target time for the labour component of the product, using the following table.

	£
Sales price per unit	30
Profit margin	12
Total costs	18
Fixed cost per unit	9
Material cost per unit	4
Maximum labour cost per unit $9+4=13-18$	5
Target labour time per unit (minutes) $\frac{1}{3}$ (of) hr	$= 20$ mins

(b) Complete the following statement:

$\frac{15.9}{20\text{mins}} = 18$ mins

$60 = 15.9$

$= .265$

$18 \times 265 = 4.77$

$\frac{159 \times 18}{60} = 4.77$

The Trade Union negotiator wished to increase the hourly labour rate by 6%. He believes that in return, employees can produce each unit in 18 minutes if they are provided with additional training. If achievable, this proposal should be **accepted** / **rejected** because it **reduces** / **increases** the labour cost per unit. The labour cost under this proposal would be

£ 4.77 per unit.

Task 2.4

Wye Limited is developing a new product and a colleague has prepared forecast information based upon two scenarios. The forecast income statement for both scenarios is shown below.

- Scenario 1 is to set the price at £15 per unit with sales of 80,000 units each year.
- Scenario 2 is to set the price at £13 per unit with sales of 120,000 units each year.

Forecast Income Statement	Scenario 1	Scenario 2
	£	£
Turnover	1,200,000	1,560,000
Cost of production		
Direct (raw) materials	240,000	360,000
Direct labour	160,000	252,000
Fixed production overheads	560,000	560,000
Total cost of sales	960,000	1,172,000
Gross profit	240,000	388,000
Selling and distribution costs	80,000	115,000
Administration costs	60,000	60,000
Operating profit	100,000	213,000
	Scenario 1	**Scenario 2**
Gross profit margin	20.00%	24.87%
Operating profit margin	8.33%	13.65%
Direct materials as a percentage of turnover	20.00%	23.08%
Direct materials cost per unit	£3.00	£3.00
Direct labour cost per unit	£2.00	£2.10
Fixed production cost per unit	£7.00	£4.67

Draft a report for the Finance Director covering the following:

(a)   An explanation of why the gross profit margins are different, referring to the following:

- Sales price and Sales volume
- Materials cost
- Labour cost
- Fixed production costs

(b)   An explanation of why the operating profit margins are different.

(c)   A recommendation, with reasons, as to which course of action to take.

---

email

To: Finance Director   Subject: Scenarios 1 & 2

From: Accounting technician   Date:

(a)   Why are the gross profit margins different?

•   Sales Price / Sales Volume

•   Materials

•   Labour

•   Fixed production costs

(b)   Why are the operating profit margins different?

(c)   Recommendation, with reasons, as to which course of action to take

Practice assessment 2

This Assessment is based on a sample assessment and subsequent amendments provided by the AAT, and is reproduced here with their kind permission.

Section 1

Task 1.1

(a) The following information has been calculated for the production of 1 unit of Beta

- Each unit will require 10 kilograms of material at a cost of £5.50 per kilogram
- Each unit will require 5 hours of labour at a total cost of £40.
- Fixed overheads total £300,000 and the estimated output will be 2,500 units of Beta

Complete the standard cost card below.

1 unit of Beta	Quantity	Cost per unit £	Total cost £
Material	10	5.5	55
Labour	5	8	40
Fixed costs		1 . .	120
Total			215

(b) An airline uses 250,000 kilograms of material to manufacture 500,000 airline meals. The standard quantity of each meal is

£ 50g

Task 1.2

1. A company purchases 10,000 kilograms of material at a cost of £33,000. The standard cost per kilogram is £3. The total material price variance is:

    ✓

(a)	£0.30	
(b)	£3,000	✓
(c)	£300	
(d)	£3.30	

2. A company uses 5,000 kilograms of material at a cost of £15,000. The budgeted production was 1,000 units, which requires 4,000 kilograms of material at a total standard cost of £14,000. The actual production was 1,000 units. The material usage variance is:

    ✓   £3 p kg

(a)	£3.50	✓
(b)	1,000 kilograms	
(c)	£3,000	
(d)	£3,500	

    $$\frac{14000}{4000}$$

3. A company uses the ideal standard to set budgets. How will this affect motivation?

    ✓

(a)	An ideal standard is easy to meet and therefore motivation will be high	
(b)	It is impossible to meet an ideal standard and therefore staff will be motivated	
(c)	An ideal standard is the highest standard and therefore staff will always achieve it	
(d)	An ideal standard is set under perfect conditions and is difficult to meet, which can demotivate staff	✓

4. A company expects to produce 12,000 units of X using 6,000 labour hours. The standard cost of labour is £14 per hour. If the actual output is 14,000 units, what is the total standard labour cost?

    ✓   ½ hr per unit

(a)	£168,000	
(b)	£98,000	✓
(c)	£196,000	
(d)	£84,000	

    Lab = 14×6000
         = 84000 for 12000 unit

    there 14000 units × ½ hr ×14
                      = 98000

Task 1.3

1. You have been given the following information:

    ■ Budgeted overheads are £600,000

    ■ Budgeted output is 25,000 units

    ■ Actual output is 30,000 units

    ■ Actual overheads are £650,000

    (handwritten: .1 × 6000 − 43000)

    (handwritten: 120 000 = 600000/25 000 = 24 = 2× × 5000)

    The fixed overhead volume variance is [FAV] **adverse / favourable**

    The fixed overhead expenditure variance is [Adv 50000] **adverse / favourable**

2. You have been given the following information: *(handwritten: 10)*

    ■ Budgeted overheads are £50,000

    ■ Budgeted output is 5,000 units and 50,000 labour hours

    ■ Actual output is 4,000 units and 43,000 actual labour hours

    ■ Actual overheads are £55,000   *(handwritten: 10000)*

    (handwritten: 50000/5000 = 10 per unit)
    (handwritten: Abs Rate Per hr 5000/50000 = 1)
    (handwritten: Budget Actual = 50000 − 43000)
    (handwritten: F over absic =)

    (handwritten: 5000 − 4000 = 1000 ×10 = 7000)

    (handwritten left margin: Fixed 50 / ACT 55)

    The fixed overhead efficiency variance is [3000] **adverse / favourable**

    (handwritten: 50000 − 43000 = 7000 × 1 abs rate)

    The fixed overhead capacity variance is [7000] **adverse / favourable**

Task 1.4

The following budgetary control report has been provided:

	Budget		Actual	
Production (bottles)		10,000		11,000
Liquid shampoo	2,500 litres	£15,000	2,800 litres	£15,400
Plastic bottles	10,000 units	£2,000	11,300 units	£2,034
Direct labour	300 hours	£3,300	350 hours	£3,325
Fixed overheads		£7,000		£7,500
Total cost		£27,300		£28,259

The following variances have been calculated:

Fixed overhead expenditure	£500 A
Direct materials (shampoo) price	£1,400 F
Direct materials (bottles) price	£226 F
Direct materials (shampoo) usage	£300 A
Direct materials (bottles) usage	£60 A
Direct labour rate	£525 F
Direct labour efficiency	£220 A
Fixed overhead volume	£700 F

Calculate the budgeted cost for 11,000 units of production. Include the variances in the appropriate part of the operating statement on the following page.

Budgeted standard cost for actual production			30030
Variances:	*Favourable*	*Adverse*	
Direct materials (shampoo) price		500	
Direct materials (shampoo) usage	1400		
Direct materials (bottles) price	226		
Direct materials (bottles) usage		300	
Direct labour rate		60	
Direct labour efficiency	525		
Fixed overhead expenditure		220	
Fixed overhead volume	700		
Total variance	2851	1080	1771
Actual cost of actual production			28259

Task 1.5

1. The table below contains the last three months cost per kilogram for product Alpha.

January	February	March
Actual price was £3.40	Actual price was £3.20	Actual price was £3.50
Seasonal variation was 20p	Seasonal variation was -0.05p	Seasonal variation was 20p

The trend in prices is an increase of £ [5p] per month.

2. A company has provided the following information:

	January	February	March
Total cost	£100,000	£120,000	£125,000
Total quantity purchased	10,000 kg	11,000 kg	10,700 kg

The cost index for March based upon January being the base period of 100 is:

(a)	107	
(b)	117	✓
(c)	125	
(d)	108	

3. The cost per unit of a product has increased from £36 in January to £40 in April. The cost per unit was £35 when the index was rebased to 100.

(a)	The cost index in April was 114 and the increase from January to April is 11.11%	✓
(b)	The cost index in April was 111 and the increase from January to April is 11.11%	
(c)	The cost index in April is 114 and the increase from January to April is 10%	
(d)	The cost index in April is 111 and the increase from January to April is 10%	

Task 1.6

You have been provided with the following operating statement for Golden Grind Limited which produces a ground coffee mix by mixing Arabica and Robusta coffee beans. *Adverse*

Variance	Favourable £	Adverse £
Direct materials (Arabica) price		£800
Direct materials (Arabica) usage	£2,250	
Direct materials (Robusta) price	£600	
Direct materials (Robusta) usage		£1,875

The Coffee Designer has given you the following information about Arabica and Robusta coffee beans:

■ Arabica beans are a higher quality and provide a richer flavour.

■ Robusta beans are considered lower quality and tend to be bitter in taste.

■ The cost of Arabica beans is set by the market and recently the price has risen sharply due to a poor harvest. The purchaser has to take the price quoted on the market. The quality of the beans was as expected.

■ The price of Robusta beans is set by the market and the price has recently fallen due to a good harvest. The purchaser has to take the price quoted on the market. The quality of the beans was as expected.

■ A mixing machine broke down resulting in disruption to the process. This led to more Robusta beans being added and less Arabica beans being added to the mix.

■ 6,000 kilograms of Robusta and 4,000 kilograms of Arabica beans were used to produce 9,500 kilograms of finished product. 500 kilograms were lost due to the machine breakdowns.

■ The breakdown has been blamed on the loss of maintenance personnel due to a lower than market pay rise.

■ In order to maintain the quality of the coffee blend, the percentage of Arabica beans should not fall below 50% of the weight of the blend.

Using this information, prepare a report to the Production Director to cover the following:

(a) Provide possible reasons for the Arabica and Robusta variances by considering the following:

■ Quality of the beans

■ Machine breakdowns

■ Mix of beans

(b)   Discuss whether the company could have taken any action, and if so, what action could have been taken in respect of the:

■   Quality of the beans

■   Machine breakdowns

---

email

to:

from:

date:

subject:

(a)   Possible reasons for the variances

■   Direct materials (Arabica) price variance

A highes quality and richer flavour £800 adverse, due to price increase because of poor crop
R lower quality tends to be better Co could not take any action since price is set by market

■   Direct materials (Arabica) usage variance

5.% of each to maintain quality

Usage variance £2,250 favourable caused by the mixing process an error of adding greater amount Robusta bean to the mix Result Co has saved money using less Arabica. But the quality may suffer and cost may complain

■   Direct materials (Robusta) price variance   Co could have

Fallen due good harvest

■   Direct materials (Robusta) usage variance   is £600 favourable This is due to market price of beans decreasing as a result of good harvest

Share price rises due to poor harvest
There is larger supply and therefore the price reduces. Co could not have taken any action since the market sets the price

(b)   Action which could have been taken

■   Quality of beans   No action as quality was as expected. quality is dependent on harvest

■   Machines breakdown

The low pay rate result in maintenance worker leaving
option 1 pay more
outsource the maintenance

Section 2

Task 2.1

Ufall has developed a skin treatment which claims to slow the ageing process. The product competes with a dozen other companies. Klineec is a major competitor and market leader, with over 60% of the market. You have been given the following information about Ufall and Klineec for the year ended 31 May 2010.

Profit and loss account	Ufall	Klineec
	£000	£000
Turnover	9,000	44,000
Cost of production		
Direct (raw) materials	2,400	6,600
Direct labour	1,500	4,400
Fixed production overheads	1,200	6,000
Total cost of sales	5,100	17,000
Gross profit	3,900	27,000
Selling and distribution costs	1,000	2,000
Administration costs	750	1,500
Advertising costs	500	20,000
Net profit	1,650	3,500

Other information		Ufall	Klineec
Number of units sold (000)	Units	1,200	4,400
Net assets	(£000)	10,000	17,000

Calculate the following performance indicators for Ufall and Klineec:

(i)   Selling price per unit

(ii)   Material cost per unit

(iii)   Labour cost per unit

(iv)   Fixed production overheads per unit

(v)   Gross profit margin

(vi)   Net profit margin

(vii)   Return on net assets

Give answers to two decimal places.

	Ufall	Klineec
Selling price per unit	£7.5	£10
Material cost per unit	£2	£1-50
Labour cost per unit	£1.25	£1
Fixed production overheads per unit	£1.00	£1-36
Gross profit margin	43%	61%
Net profit margin	18%	8%
Advertising cost as % of turnover	5.5%	45.5%
Return on net assets	17%	21%

$$\frac{9000}{1200}$$

$$\frac{2400}{1200}$$

.500

$$\frac{44000}{4400}$$

6600

4400
4450
4400

Task 2.2

Alpha Limited manufactures an anti-aging cream and is considering how it can be more environmentally friendly. Scientists have developed a new product to replace Alpha's existing anti-ageing cream; the new product is a solid bar and takes up less than 10% of the volume and weight of the existing product.

You have been given the following information.

■   Current sales volume is 1.2 million units per annum and this is not expected to change.

■   Current fixed production costs are £1.2 million.

■   Current labour cost per unit is £1.25 which is completely variable.

■   Current material cost per unit is £2 and is completely variable.

■   Assume stock levels are kept at zero.

■   Variable material cost of the new product will be £0.50 less per unit than the current cream.

■   Selling price will be increased from £7.50 to £8.50.

■   Fixed selling and distribution costs will reduce from £1,000,000 to £400,000.

■   Additional investment in assets will be £3 million which will be depreciated at £500,000 per annum.

■   All other costs will remain the same.

(a)   Calculate the total annual increase in profit by completing the table below.

	Units	Price/cost £	Total £
Additional revenue	1200000	1	1200000
Savings on materials		·5	600000
Reduction in selling and distribution costs			600000
Additional depreciation			500000
Additional annual profit			1900000

(b) The return on the additional investment is $\boxed{63.33}$ % $\dfrac{1\,900\,000}{3\,000\,000}$

(c) The marketing department is concerned that the volume of sales may not reach 1.2 million. The finance director has asked for the break even sales volume.

The fixed costs are   £ $\boxed{2\,100\,000}$

$\text{Fixed cost} \quad \overset{\text{Fixed cost}}{1\,200\,000} + \overset{\text{dep}}{500\,000} + \overset{\text{set up cost}}{400\,000}$

The contribution per unit is   £ $\boxed{5.75}$

$8-50 = (\cdots \underset{1.25 \times 2}{\text{current lab mat}})\; 3.25 - 50p = 2.75$
$= 5.75$

The break even sales volume is $\boxed{365217}$ units

$\dfrac{2\,100\,000}{5.75}$

Task 2.3

Alpha Limited will be replacing some machines in the next year and needs to decide whether to purchase or lease the machines.

The discount factors you will need for task 2.3 (a) and (b) are shown below.

Year	Discount factor 5%	Year	Discount factor 5%
0	1.00	3	0.864
1	0.952	4	0.823
2	0.907	5	0.784

(a) Calculate the discounted lifecycle cost of purchasing the machine based upon the following:

■ Purchase price of £500,000

■ Annual running costs of £40,000 for the next five years, paid annually in arrears

■ A residual value of £200,000 at the end of the five years

Year	0	1	2	3	4	5
Cash flow	500000	40000	40000	40000	40000	160000 40000
Discount factor		.952	.907	.864	.823	.784
Present value		38080	36280	34560	32920	31360
Net present cost						

(b) Calculate the discounted lifecycle cost of leasing the machine for five years based upon the total annual costs of £125,000 paid annually in advance.

Year	0	1	2	3	4
Lease costs	125000	125000	125000	125000	125000
Discount factor	1.00	.952	.907	.864	.823
Present value	125000 500000	119000	113375	108000	102875
Net present cost	568 250				

(c) Based on the calculations it is best to **purchase / lease** the machine, which saves

£ _____

for your calculations:

Task 2.4

A division of Alpha Limited is developing a new product and a colleague has prepared forecast information based upon two scenarios. The forecast income statement and statement of financial position for both scenarios are shown below.

■ Scenario 1 is to set the price at £9 per unit with sales of 120,000 units each year.

■ Scenario 2 is to set the price at £6 per unit with sales of 240,000 units each year.

Forecast income statement	Scenario 1	Scenario 2
	£	£
Turnover	1,080,000	1,440,000
Cost of production		
Direct (raw) materials	300,000	600,000
Direct labour	120,000	192,000
Fixed production overheads	360,000	360,000
Total cost of sales	780,000	1,152,000
Gross profit	**300,000**	**288,000**
Selling and distribution costs	74,000	122,000
Administration costs	50,000	50,000
Operating profit	**176,000**	**116,000**
	Scenario 1	**Scenario 2**
Gross profit margin	27.78%	20.00%
Operating profit margin	16.30%	8.06%
Direct materials as a percentage of turnover	27.78%	41.67%
Direct materials cost per unit	£2.50	£2.50
Direct labour cost per unit	£1.00	£0.80
Fixed production cost per unit	£3.00	£1.50

Draft a report for the Finance Director covering the following:

(a) An explanation of why the gross profit margins are different, referring to the following:

■ Sales price

■ Sales volume

■ Materials

■ Labour

■ Fixed costs

■ The dominant factor

    (b)   An explanation of why the net profit margins are different.

    (c)   A recommendation, with reasons, as to which course of action to take.

---

email

to:

from:

date:

subject:

(a)   Why are the gross profit margins different?

      ■   Sales Price / Sales Volume

      ■   Materials

      ■   Labour

      ■   Fixed costs

      ■   Which is the dominant factor and why?

(b)   Why are the net profit margins different?

(c)   Recommendation, with reasons, as to which course of action to take.

Practice assessment 3

Section 1

Task 1.1

The following information has been provided related to the production of Quintox.

- Fixed overheads are absorbed on a per unit basis.

- The budgeted output per month is 500,000 units of Quintox.

- During December there was over-absorption of fixed overheads of £25,000.

- Actual fixed overheads in December amounted to £551,000.

- The actual output of Quintox in December was 480,000 units.

Calculate the information required to complete the following table:

Fixed overhead absorbed in December	£ 576000
Fixed overhead absorption rate per unit	£ 1.20
Budgeted total fixed overheads per month	£ 600000

Handwritten annotations:

551
25

5000000 × 1.2 = 600 000

576000 × 1.2 = 600000
────────
480000

A

mat varian 8900 Sp M x7 × 57000 = 1000 A
52500/75 0
Direct mat usage (1650 × 3 sqm) -800
= 350 A
Direct labour rate (2800 × 15)
7500 Sq m / 2500 = 3

Direct Labour Rate Variance

(2800 × 15) - 42000 = 0
37500 = 15
────
250)

Direct labour eff
(26500y 1 hr per unit) - 2800 × 15
= 2250

Task 1.2

Classy Glass Limited manufactures sealed triple-glazed units for new energy-efficient houses.

The company operates a standard cost system in which:

■   Purchases of materials are recorded at standard cost

■   Direct material and direct labour costs are variable

■   Production overheads are fixed and absorbed on a labour hour basis

The budgeted activity and actual results for the month of March are as follows:

	Budget		Actual	
Production (sealed units)		2,500		2,650
Direct materials (glass)	7,500 sq m 7	£52,500	8,000 sq m	£57,000
Direct labour	2,500 hours	£37,500	2,800 hours	£42,000
Fixed overheads		£75,000		£74,000
Total cost		£165,000		£173,000

(a)   Calculate the following variances (if any) for March:

Variance	£	A/F
Direct material price variance	1000	A
Direct material usage variance	3 50	A
Direct labour rate variance	0	
Direct labour efficiency variance	2250	A

(b)   It has been revealed that the direct labour force is not yet fully trained. It is estimated that this would account for each unit taking 5% longer than standard to manufacture.

Calculate the part of the direct labour efficiency variance related to training, and the part that may be due to other factors.

Variance	£	A/F
Part of direct labour efficiency variance due to incomplete training	1987-50	A
Part of direct labour efficiency variance due to other factors	262.50	A

2650 bunts × 1·05 = 2782-50

direct labour efficiency varié due to training

= 2650 — 2782-50 × 15 = 1987-50 A

Labour labour eff due to other factor

2782-50 — 2800 × 15 = 262·50 A

Task 1.3

You have been provided with the following information regarding fixed overheads:

Budgeted fixed overheads	£600,000
Fixed overhead absorption base	Direct labour hours
Budgeted output	300,000 units
Standard labour hours per unit	0.2 hours
Actual output	285,000 units
Actual labour hours	55,000 hours
Actual fixed overheads	£612,000

2 (handwritten next to Budgeted output row)

60000 (handwritten next to Actual labour hours row)

Calculate the following information and insert the figures into the table

	£	A / F
Fixed overhead absorption rate per direct labour hour	10	
Fixed overhead expenditure variance	12000	A
Fixed overhead absorbed by actual production	570000	
Fixed overhead volume variance	30000	A
Fixed overhead capacity variance	50000	A
Fixed overhead efficiency variance	20000	A

(handwritten working below:)

① FIXED O/H Absorb 600000 (300000 × .2 = £10 pu hr

② Fixed overhead exp variance -600000 -612000

③ Fixed overhead absorb by actual prod   St hr for act prod = 285000 × .2 = 57000

   - 57000 × £10   = 570 000

④ Fixed overhead volume variance 570000 - 600000 = 30000 A

⑤ Fixed overhead cap variance (55000 × £10) - 600000 = 50 000 A

⑥ Fixed efficiency variance 570000 - 550 000 = 20000 A

Task 1.4

A company uses standard marginal costing to monitor and control its costs. The company's only product is milk which is purchased in bulk and sold in 2 litre bottles. The milk, bottles and direct labour are all variable costs. Fixed overheads are the only fixed costs.

The following budgetary control report has been provided:

	Budget		**Actual**	
Production (bottles)		4,000,000		3,950,000
Milk	8,000,000 litres	£3,200,000	7,905,000 litres	£3,122,500
Bottles	4,000,000 units	£60,000	3,950,800 units	£60,100
Direct labour	2,000 hours	£36,000	2,000 hours	£36,500
Fixed overheads		£400,000		£401,500
Total costs		£3,696,000		£3,620,600

The following variances have been calculated:

Direct materials (milk) price	£39,500	F
Direct materials (milk) usage	£2,000	
Direct materials (bottles) price	£838	A
Direct materials (bottles) usage	£12	A
Direct labour rate	£500	A
Direct labour efficiency	£450	A
Fixed overhead expenditure	£1,500	A

Complete the marginal costing operating statement on the next page.

Budgeted/standard variable cost for actual production			3254 800
Budgeted fixed costs			400 000
Variances	**Favourable**	**Adverse**	
Direct materials (milk) price	39500	~~39500~~	
Direct materials (milk) usage		2000	
Direct materials (bottles) price		838 A	
Direct materials (bottles) usage		12	
Direct labour rate		500	
Direct labour efficiency		450	
Fixed overhead expenditure		1500	
Total variance	34200 ~~39500~~		
Actual cost of actual production			3620600

$$(= 3200000 + 6000 + 36000) \checkmark$$

$$\frac{3951\,000}{400000}$$

$$= 3254800$$

$$= 3296000$$

Task 1.5

(a) The following data relates to the prices per kilogram of a type of fruit. Complete the table by inserting the seasonal variations, including + or – signs.

	March	April	May
Actual price	£1.30	£1.25	£1.10
Trend	£1.28 ·2	£1.30 ·5	£1.32 +22
Seasonal variation	– ·02	+ ·05	+·22

(b) A formula has been developed to estimate the future trend in vehicle prices.

It is based on the equation y = mx + c, where   =33 x25 + 14000

y is the expected price for a specific type of vehicle in the future

m is a constant £25

x is the month number of the required future date, counting from the base month of January 2012 (ie January 2012 is month 0)

c is a constant £14,000

Calculate the expected vehicle price in October 2014.

£ 14825

(c) Calculate the 3 month moving averages for the following sales volume data:

Month	Sales volume	3 month moving average
January	57,000	
February	58,000	57500
March	57,500	58 500
April	60,000	59 500
May	61,000	60 500
June	60,500	61 500
July	63,000	

Task 1.6

Performance Assemblies Limited reconditions and tunes vehicle engines for sale to the motor trade.

The company uses two grades of direct labour. Grade L employees are paid a basic £13 per hour and normally carry out the basic assembly of the reconditioned engines. Grade H employees are those who have been promoted from grade L and given further training to enable them to carry out the more advanced assembly work together with engine tuning. Grade H employees are paid a basic £17 per hour. Both grades of employee are paid a 50% premium rate for any overtime, and this is incorporated into the actual direct labour cost. The standard hourly rates have been set at £14 for grade L and £18 for grade H employees to allow for a small amount of premium rate pay.

During the month of May the following variances were recorded.

Variance	Favourable £	Adverse £
Direct labour (Grade L) efficiency	£7,700	
Direct labour (Grade L) rate	£1,450	
Direct labour (Grade H) efficiency		£9,000
Direct labour (Grade H) rate		£3,875

You have discovered the following additional information regarding the May results.

■   The standard labour hours for the actual output during May was 2,000 hours of grade L labour plus 2,000 hours of grade H labour.

■   Several grade L employees were sick during May.

■   No grade L employees worked any overtime in May.

■   Several grade H employees agreed to carry out duties normally carried out by grade L employees during May. This was in addition to their normal hours, and increased their usual amount of overtime hours.

Using this information, prepare a report for the Production Director providing an explanation of each variance together with possible reasons for each variance (including numerical information where possible).

$$\frac{7700}{14} = 550 \ \text{hrs}$$

$$\frac{9000}{18} = 500 \ \text{hrs}$$

Direct Labour Variances for May – Explanations and Possible Reasons

■   Direct labour (Grade L) efficiency variance

■   Direct labour (Grade L) rate variance

■   Direct labour (Grade H) efficiency variance

■   Direct labour (Grade H) rate variance

Section 2

Task 2.1

Eye Limited is comparing its results with its major competitor Jay plc. You have been given the following information about Eye and Jay for the year just ended.

Income Statement	Eye	Jay
	£000	£000
Turnover	36,000	57,200
Cost of production		
Direct (raw) materials	8,000	13,650
Direct labour	7,200	11,375
Fixed production overheads	5,000	9,000
Total cost of production	20,200	34,025
Gross profit	**15,800**	**23,175**
Selling and distribution costs	4,000	7,100
Administration costs	3,250	4,800
Advertising costs	4,200	5,500
Net profit	**4,350**	**5,775**

Other information		Eye	Jay
Number of units sold	Units	4,000,000	6,500,000
Net assets	(£000)	65,000	95,000

Calculate the performance indicators to complete the following table for Eye Ltd and Jay plc:

Give answers to two decimal places.

	Eye Ltd	Jay plc
Selling price per unit	£9	£8-80
Direct material cost per unit	£2	
Direct labour cost per unit		
Fixed production overheads per unit		
Gross profit margin		
Net profit margin		
Administration cost as % of turnover		
Return on net assets		

Task 2.2

Tripro Limited manufactures three products, the Uno, Duo and Trio. The following statement shows the draft budget for the following three months.

	Uno	Duo	Trio	Total
Sales (units)	200,000	150,000	250,000	
	£	£	£	£
Sales Revenue	2,000,000	750,000	3,000,000	5,750,000
Materials	500,000	250,000	1,250,000	2,000,000
Labour	400,000	400,000	400,000	1,200,000
Overheads	300,000	300,000	300,000	900,000
Profit / (Loss)	800,000	(200,000)	1,050,000	1,650,000

You have established the following facts about the business.

■   The same type of material is used for each product, at a cost of £10 per kilo.

■   The products are made in one factory.

■   The employees are all paid a fixed salary, and are on annual contracts which have just been renewed. The total labour cost is apportioned in the budget evenly over the three products.

■   The overheads are a fixed cost which has been spread evenly over the three products in the budget.

The material supplier has just notified the company that the supply will be restricted in the next three months to 150,000 kilos. Tripro Limited does not hold any inventory of this material.

Draft a revised budget using the following format that maximises the profit that can be achieved based on the restricted volume of raw material.

	Uno	Duo	Trio	Total
Sales (units)				
	£	£	£	£
Sales Revenue				
Materials				
Contribution				
Labour				
Overheads				
Profit				

Task 2.3

Star Assemblies Limited is considering installing a new boiler system in its factory to provide heating and power.

Details are as follows:

- The existing boiler system will cost £8,000 to remove, and has no value. If retained, the existing boiler system has an expected life of a further 5 years.

- The new boiler system will cost £57,000 including installation.

- The current boiler system costs £22,000 per year in energy, £8,000 per year in maintenance and £2,000 per year in depreciation.

- The new boiler system would cost £12,000 per year in energy, cost nothing to maintain in the first two years (as it would be under guarantee) and £3,000 per year for the remaining life.

- The new boiler would be depreciated in the accounts on a straight line basis over the life of 5 years. There is no expected residual value.

- At the end of the 5 year period both old and new boiler systems would have the same cost of removal.

- The company's cost of capital is 10%, and this rate has been used for the discount factors in the table shown below.

- All annual costs can be assumed to occur in arrears.

(a) Complete the following table to calculate the net present value of the new system.

Year	Detail	Cash Flow £	Discount Factor	Present Value £
0	Initial costs		1.000	
1	Net annual savings		0.909	
2			0.826	
3			0.751	
4			0.683	
5			0.621	
Net Present Value				

(b) Complete the following sentence.

The net present value of the scheme is **positive / negative**, so from a financial point of view the new boiler system is **worthwhile / not worthwhile**.

for your calculations:

Task 2.4

Vista Hotels Limited operates a number of small hotels. As part of its planning process it is considering following one of two scenarios for the next year.

Income Statement	Scenario 1	Scenario 2
	£	£
Turnover	1,200,000	1,950,000
Variable costs		
Food	150,000	300,000
Laundry	105,000	210,000
Cleaning	180,000	300,000
Total variable costs	435,000	810,000
Contribution	**765,000**	**1,140,000**
Selling and marketing costs	100,000	450,000
Administration costs	350,000	350,000
Financial costs	130,000	130,000
Net profit	**185,000**	**210,000**

Other information

Number of room-nights occupied	15,000	30,000
Number of room-nights available	40,000	40,000

The first scenario is based on the current situation. The second scenario is based on using a combination of discounting and advertising with celebrity endorsement.

Draft a report to the Finance Director covering the following

■   An explanation of why the contribution amounts are different

■   An explanation of why the net profit margins and amounts are different

■   A recommendation, with reasons, as to which scenario to adopt

Report on Scenarios

■   Contribution Amounts

■   Net Profit Margins and Amounts

■   Recommendation, with reasons

Practice assessment 1 – answers

Task 1.1

(a)

1 unit of Exe	Quantity	Cost per unit £	Total cost £
Material	1.3	4.50	5.85
Labour	0.2	18.00	3.60
Fixed costs	0.2	10.00	2.00
Total			11.45

(b) The standard quantity of material for each unit is 0.2kg

Task 1.2

1. (a) £720 Favourable

2. (c) £800 Adverse

3. (c) £125,000

4. (b) £3,300 Adverse

Task 1.3

(a) The fixed overhead volume variance is £20,000 **favourable.**

The fixed overhead expenditure variance is £15,000 **adverse.**

(b) The fixed overhead efficiency variance is £2,700 **adverse.**

The fixed overhead capacity variance is £900 **adverse.**

Task 1.4

Budgeted cost for actual production			77,868
Variances:	Favourable	Adverse	
Direct materials (instant coffee) price		310	
Direct materials (instant coffee) usage		150	
Direct materials (glass jars) price	18		
Direct materials (glass jars) usage		8	
Direct labour rate	110		
Direct labour efficiency		252	
Fixed overhead expenditure		150	
Fixed overhead volume	300		
Total variances	428	870	**442**
Actual cost of actual production			**78,310**

Task 1.5

1. The trend in prices is an **increase** of £0.60 per month.

2. (d)   106

3. (b)   The cost index in April was 122 and the decrease from January to April is 2.4%

Task 1.6

email	
to: Production Director	from: Accounting technician
date: xx/xx/xxxx	subject: Report on September production of strawberry yoghurt

There were three significant material variances.

Price Variances

*   Explanation and reasons

    The only significant price variance was an adverse variance of £30,000 relating to the price of strawberries. This appears to have been caused by the poor UK weather which increased the buying price from the standard 50p per kg to an average 60p per kg. The actual quantity of strawberries used per pot was 150 grams (as identified below under 'Usage Variances'), therefore the actual quantity used in 2 million pots was 300,000 kilos. This accounts for the price variance of £30,000.

*   Future strategies

    Although such price changes caused by weather conditions are difficult to avoid, the buyer could consider sourcing fruit from outside the UK if necessary. This would however have transport cost implications and would have to be considered carefully so as not to damage our relationships with our current suppliers.

Usage Variances

*   Explanation and reasons

    There was an adverse usage variance of £50,000 for strawberries, and a favourable usage variance of £20,000 for yoghurt. Both these variances relate to the malfunction of the filling equipment.

    It seems from the data that the equipment filled each 500 gram pot with an average of 350 grams of yoghurt and 150 grams of strawberries. The additional 50 grams of strawberries at the standard price of 50p per kilo for the 2 million pots accounts for the £50,000 variance. The favourable variance for the reduced amount of yoghurt is lower at £20,000 since the yoghurt is cheaper at a standard 20p per kilo.

    Although this malfunction would not have created any legal issues since the fruit content was well above the minimum stated on the pots, we have incurred additional net costs of £30,000.

*   Future strategies

    Urgent consideration should be given to regular quality checks on the output of all the production lines (for example hourly). This could be carried out using sampling to analyse the content of the output so that any equipment malfunction is quickly noticed and action taken. Simply weighing each pot is not sufficient, since this does not detect a problem of the kind that has occurred in September.

If you require any further information, please contact me.

Section 2

Task 2.1

	Cosy	Lush
Selling price per room-night	£75.00	£70.00
Occupancy rate (%)	50.00%	80.00%
Variable costs per room-night	£40.00	£35.00
Contribution per room-night	£35.00	£35.00
Contribution / sales ratio (%)	46.67%	50.00%
Net profit margin	5.52%	12.44%
Selling and marketing cost as % of turnover	22.86%	20.83%

Task 2.2

(a)

	Units	Price/cost £	Total £
Additional revenue	3,000,000	0.10	300,000
Savings on materials	3,000,000	0.15	450,000
Reduction in selling and distribution costs			150,000
Additional depreciation			(400,00)
Additional annual profit			500,000

(b)

Return on additional investment (%)	12.5%
Total fixed costs	£1,350,000
Contribution per unit	£1.35
Break even sales volume in units	1,000,000
Margin of safety (%)	66.67%

Task 2.3

(a)

	£
Sales price per unit	30.00
Profit margin	12.00
Total costs	18.00
Fixed cost per unit	9.00
Material cost per unit	4.00
Maximum labour cost per unit	5.00
Target labour time per unit (minutes)	20

(b)   The Trade Union negotiator wished to increase the hourly labour rate by 6%. He believes that in return, employees can produce each unit in 18 minutes if they are provided with additional training. If achievable, this proposal should be **accepted** because it **reduces** the labour cost per unit. The labour cost under this proposal would be **£4.77** per unit.

Task 2.4

---

email

To: Finance Director   Subject: Scenarios 1 & 2

From: Accounting technician   Date:

(a)   Why are the gross profit margins different?

•   Sales Price / Sales Volume

Although the sales volume in scenario 2 is 50% greater than in scenario 1, this itself does not affect the gross profit margin (as a percentage). As noted later the increased volume does however spread the fixed costs over more units. The margin is affected by the selling price which is £2 per unit less in scenario 2. This has the effect of reducing the gross profit margin as a percentage.

•   Materials

The material cost is the same per unit in each scenario, since it behaves as a variable cost. This therefore has no impact on the gross profit margin.

•   Labour

The labour cost per unit is slightly higher when the volume is greater. This could be due (for example) to the use of overtime working. The impact on the gross profit margin is to reduce it slightly in scenario 2.

•   Fixed production costs

The fixed production costs form a large part of the cost of production. Since the volume is much higher in scenario 2, the fixed production cost per unit is significantly lower. This has the effect of improving the gross profit margin, and is the main factor in the difference between the margins. It more than compensates for the impact of selling price and labour costs.

(b)   Why are the operating profit margins different?

The operating profit margin in scenario 2 is influenced by the gross profit margin which is better than that in scenario 1, as discussed above. It also benefits from selling and distribution costs that appear to be semi-variable, and administration costs that behave as a fixed cost.

(c)   Recommendation, with reasons, as to which course of action to take

Provided the situation outlined in scenario 2 is thought to be achievable, then this should be followed, since it provides more than twice the operating profit of scenario 1. This is due to the economies of scale that impact on the fixed costs within the business.

However, before finalising a decision, particular care should be taken to examine the sales units forecast under scenario 2, because if this is flawed then the selling price reduction could easily lead to a worse operating profit than in scenario 1.

Practice assessment 2
– answers

Task 1.1

(a)

1 unit of Beta	Quantity	Cost per unit £	Total cost £
Material	10	5.50	55
Labour	5	8	40
Fixed costs	1 (accept 5 hours)	120 (24 per hour)	120
Total			215

(b) The standard quantity of each meal is £0.50

Task 1.2

1. (b) £3,000

2. (d) £3,500

3. (d) An ideal standard is set under perfect conditions and is difficult to meet, which can demotivate staff

4. (b) £98,000

Task 1.3

1. The fixed overhead volume variance is 120,000 **favourable**

   The fixed overhead expenditure variance is 50,000 **adverse**

2. The fixed overhead efficiency variance is 3,000 **adverse**

   The fixed overhead capacity variance is 7,000 **adverse**

Task 1.4

Budgeted standard cost for actual production			£30,030
Variances:	Favourable	Adverse	
Direct materials (shampoo) price	£1,400		
Direct materials (shampoo) usage		£300	
Direct materials (bottles) price	£226		
Direct materials (bottles) usage		£60	
Direct labour rate	£525		
Direct labour efficiency		£220	
Fixed overhead expenditure		£500	
Fixed overhead volume	£700		
Total variance	£2,851	£1,080	£1,771
Actual cost of actual production			£28,259

Task 1.5

1. The trend in prices is an increase of £0.05 per month.

2. The cost index for March based upon January being the base period of 100 is: **(b)**   117

3. **(a)**   The cost index in April was 114 and the increase from January to April is 11.11%

Task 1.6

email	
To: Production Director	Subject: Reason for variances
From: AAT student	Date: xx/xx/xxxx

(a)   Possible reasons for the variances

· Direct materials (Arabica) price variance

The price variance for Arabica beans is £800 adverse. This is due to the market price of beans increasing due to the poor harvest, meaning there is lower supply, and so the price increases. The company could not have taken any action as the market sets the price.

· Direct materials (Arabica) usage variance

The usage variance for Arabica beans is £2,250 favourable. This has been caused by the mixing process making an error and adding a greater amount of Robusta beans to the mix. The result is that the company has saved money because they have used less Arabica beans per kilogram of production, but the mix is outside of the range recommended to produce an acceptable quality blend. Therefore the customers may be unhappy.

The company could have secured the maintenance personnel by paying a market rate.

· Direct materials (Robusta) price variance

The price variance for Robusta beans is £600 favourable. This is due to the market price of beans decreasing as a result of a good harvest, meaning there is a larger supply, and so the price reduces. The company could not have taken any action as the market sets the price.

· Direct materials (Robusta) usage variance

The usage variance is £1,875 adverse because the company used more beans than expected. This was because of the mixing machine breaking down.

(b)   Action which could have been taken

· Quality of beans

No action is necessary. As the quality was as expected, no action could be taken as quality is dependent on the harvest.

· Machines breakdown

The information states that the low pay rise meant that maintenance staff left. One option would be to pay more to retain maintenance staff, or to outsource to a reliable company.

Section 2

Task 2.1

	Ufall	Klineec
Selling price per unit	£7.50	£10.00
Material cost per unit	£2.00	£1.50
Labour cost per unit	£1.25	£1.00
Fixed production overheads per unit	£1.00	£1.36
Gross profit margin	43%	61%
Net profit margin	18%	8%
Advertising cost as % of turnover	5.6%	45.5%
Return on net assets	17%	21%

Task 2.2

(a)

	Units	Price/cost £	Total £
Additional revenue	1,200,000	£1	1,200,000
Savings on materials	1,200,000	0.5	600,000
Reduction in selling and distribution costs			600,000
Additional depreciation			–500,000
Additional annual profit			1,900,000

(b) Additional investment / Additional assets = £1,900,000 / £3,000,000 = 63.33%

(c) The fixed costs are £1.2 million plus £400,000 plus additional depreciation of £500,000 = **£2.1 million.**

The contribution per unit is £8.50 less (3.25 – 0.50) = 8.50 – 2.75 = **£5.75 per unit.**

The break even sales volume is **365,218 units**.

Task 2.3

(a)

Year	0	1	2	3	4	5
Cash Flow	£500,000	£40,000	£40,000	£40,000	£40,000	−£160,000
Discount factor	1	0.952	0.907	0.864	0.823	0.784
Present value	£500,000	£38,080	£36,280	£34,560	£32,920	−£125,440
Net present cost	£516,400					

(b)

Year	0	1	2	3	4
Lease costs	£125,000	£125,000	£125,000	£125,000	£125,000
Discount factor	1	0.952	0.907	0.864	0.823
Present value	£125,000	£119,000	£113,375	£108,000	£102,875
Net present cost	£568,250				

(c)   Based on the calculations it is best to **purchase** the machine, which saves **£51,850**.

Task 2.4

email	
To: Finance director	Subject: various
From: Accounting technician	Date: xx/xx/xx

(a)   **Why are the gross profit margins different?**

- Sales Price / Sales Volume

  The sales price is higher under Scenario 1, which will result in an increase in the gross profit margin. However, the sales volume is half that of Scenario 2, which will reduce the margin if there are fixed costs because the fixed cost per unit will be higher.

- Materials

  The materials cost per unit is constant and therefore does not affect the gross profit margin. There is no economy of scale.

- Labour

  Labour cost per unit is £1 for Scenario 1 decreasing to £0.80 for Scenario 2. The more units that are produced, the lower the labour cost per unit. This will improve the margin for Scenario 2. It may be because of economies of scale in production or the learning effect.

- Fixed costs

  Fixed costs are constant in total, and so as the volume of production increases, the fixed cost per unit decreases. This will increase the margin.

- Which is the dominant factor and why?

  Scenario 2 sells twice as many units as Scenario 1, has the same material cost per unit, lower labour cost per unit, and lower fixed costs per unit. All of these would increase Scenario 2's margin. However, the margin is lower. This is due to the lower sales price per unit, which is the dominant factor.

(b)   **Why are the net profit margins different?**

The net profit margins are different partly due to the reduction in gross profit for Scenario 2, and partly due to the increased sales and distribution costs in Scenario 2.

(c)   **Recommendation, with reasons, as to which course of action to take**

Based purely on the forecast information, Scenario 1 is the best option creating the largest return. However, the sales volume is lower than Scenario 2, and so the market share is lower. It may be worth setting the price lower to gain market share. Alternatively, what would be the demand if the price could be set at approximately £8 per unit?

Practice assessment 3 – answers

Section 1

Task 1.1

Fixed overhead absorbed in December	£576,000
Fixed overhead absorption rate per unit	£1.20
Budgeted total fixed overheads per month	£600,000

Workings:

Fixed overheads absorbed in December:

Actual overheads £551,000 + Over-absorption £25,000 = £576,000

Fixed overhead absorption rate per unit:

Fixed overheads absorbed £576,000 ÷ Actual units produced 480,000 = £1.20

Budgeted total fixed overheads per month:

Budgeted output per month 500,000 units x Absorption rate £1.20 = £600,000

Task 1.2

(a)

Variance	£	A/F
Direct material price variance	1,000	A
Direct material usage variance	350	A
Direct labour rate variance	0	
Direct labour efficiency variance	2,250	A

Workings:

Direct materials price variance
(8,000 sq m x £7*) - £57,000 = £1,000 A
        *£52,500 / 7,500 sq m

Direct materials usage variance
((2,650 x 3 sq m*) – 8,000 sq m) x £7 = £350 A
        *7,500 sq m / 2,500 units

Direct labour rate variance
(2,800 x £15*) - £42,000 = £0
        *£37,500 / 2,500 hours

Direct labour efficiency variance
((2,650 units x 1 hour per unit) – 2,800 hours) x £15 = £2,250 A

(b)

Variance	£	A/F
Part of direct labour efficiency variance due to incomplete training	1,987.50	A
Part of direct labour efficiency variance due to other factors	262.50	A

Workings:

Revised time to make 2,650 units:
2,650 x 1.05 hours = 2,782.5 hours

Direct labour efficiency variance due to training
(2,650 hours – 2,782.5 hours) x £15 = £1,987.50 A

Direct labour efficiency variance due to other factors
(2,782.5 hours – 2,800 hours) x £15 = £262.50 A

Task 1.3

	£	A / F
Fixed overhead absorption rate per direct labour hour	10	
Fixed overhead expenditure variance	12,000	A
Fixed overhead absorbed by actual production	570,000	
Fixed overhead volume variance	30,000	A
Fixed overhead capacity variance	50,000	A
Fixed overhead efficiency variance	20,000	F

Workings:

Fixed overhead absorption rate per direct labour hour
£600,000 / (300,000 units x 0.2 hours) = £10

Fixed overhead expenditure variance
£600,000 - £612,000 = £12,000 A

Fixed overhead absorbed by actual production
Standard hours for actual production: 285,000 units x 0.2 = 57,000 hours
Overhead absorbed: 57,000 hours x £10 = £570,000

Fixed overhead volume variance
£570,000 - £600,000 = £30,000 A

Fixed overhead capacity variance
(55,000 x £10) - £600,000 = £50,000 A

Fixed overhead efficiency variance
£570,000 - £550,000 = £20,000 F

Task 1.4

Budgeted/standard variable cost for actual production			3,254,800
Budgeted fixed costs			**400,000**
Variances	**Favourable**	**Adverse**	
Direct materials (milk) price	39,500		
Direct materials (milk) usage		2,000	
Direct materials (bottles) price		838	
Direct materials (bottles) usage		12	
Direct labour rate		500	
Direct labour efficiency		450	
Fixed overhead expenditure		1,500	
Total variance	34,200		- 34,200
Actual cost of actual production			3,620,600

Working:

Budgeted / Standard variable cost for actual production

(£3,200,000 + £60,000 + £36,000) x 3,950,000 / 4,000,000 = £3,254,800

Task 1.5

(a)

	March	April	May
Actual price	£1.30	£1.25	£1.10
Trend	£1.28	£1.30	£1.32
Seasonal variation	+£0.02	-£0.05	-£0.22

(b) **£14,825**

Working: y = (£25 x 33) + £14,000

(c)

Month	Sales volume	3 month moving average
January	57,000	
February	58,000	57,500
March	57,500	58,500
April	60,000	59,500
May	61,000	60,500
June	60,500	61,500
July	63,000	

Task 1.6

Direct Labour Variances for May – Explanations and Possible Reasons

■ Direct labour (Grade L) efficiency variance

The labour efficiency variance is the result of more or fewer hours being taken than the standard number for the output. The difference in hours is valued at the standard hourly rate. In this case the variance of £7,700 favourable means that 550 fewer hours than the standard 2,000 hours were worked, valued at the standard £14 per hour.

This may have been caused by the absence of some grade L workers during May, whose work was then undertaken by grade H employees.

■ Direct labour (Grade L) rate variance

The labour rate variance shows the increased or reduced cost of the actual hours worked due to paying a rate that differs from standard. Here the actual 1,450 hours worked have cost £1,450 less than if they had been paid at the standard rate of £14 per hour. This means that the actual rate was the basic £13 per hour, which agrees with the fact that there was no overtime premium rates paid to this level of employees during May.

■ Direct labour (Grade H) efficiency variance

The adverse efficiency variance of £9,000 for grade H employees is a reflection of the increased number of hours worked during May compared to standard. This equates to an additional 500 hours at the standard rate of £18 per hour. It is likely that this is mainly due to grade H employees undertaking work normally carried out by grade L employees. However if we examine the total hours worked by both grades we find that 1,450 + 2,500 = 3,950 hours were worked, which is slightly fewer than the 4,000 standard hours. This could possibly be due to the higher grade employees working more quickly on the lower level work.

■ Direct labour (Grade H) rate variance

The adverse variance of £3,875 relates to the additional cost of paying the actual hours at an average rate that is higher than the standard £18 per hour. This is probably due to the overtime premium rate that was paid during May so that grade H employees could carry out the additional work normally carried out by grade L employees. If more overtime than normal is worked the proportion of hours paid at the higher rate of £25.50 will be greater, increasing the labour cost.

Section 2

Task 2.1

	Eye Ltd	Jay plc
Selling price per unit	£9.00	£8.80
Direct material cost per unit	£2.00	£2.10
Direct labour cost per unit	£1.80	£1.75
Fixed production overheads per unit	£1.25	£1.38
Gross profit margin	43.89%	40.52%
Net profit margin	12.08%	10.10%
Administration cost as % of turnover	9.03%	8.39%
Return on net assets	6.69%	6.08%

Task 2.2

	Uno	Duo	Trio	Total
Sales (units)	200,000	150,000	150,000	
	£	£	£	£
Sales Revenue	2,000,000	750,000	1,800,000	4,550,000
Materials	500,000	250,000	750,000	1,500,000
Contribution	1,500,000	500,000	1,050,000	3,050,000
Labour				1,200,000
Overheads				900,000
Profit				950,000

Workings:

Priority should be given to the products with the highest contribution per kilo of raw material. This is calculated as follows:

	Uno	Duo	Trio
Contribution			
(Sales revenue – materials)	£1,500,000	£500,000	£1,750,000
Materials required (kilos)	50,000	25,000	125,000
Contribution per kilo	£30	£20	£14

Therefore priority should be given to Uno and Duo, with the balance of available material being used to make Trios. Each unit of Trio requires 0.5 kilos of material (125,000 kilos / 250,000 units). The remaining 75,000 kilos of material now available is enough to make 75,000 / 0.5 = 150,000 units of Trio.

Task 2.3

(a)

Year	Detail	Cash Flow £	Discount Factor	Present Value £
0	Initial costs	-65,000	1.000	-65,000
1	Net annual savings	18,000	0.909	16,362
2		18,000	0.826	14,868
3		15,000	0.751	11,265
4		15,000	0.683	10,245
5		15,000	0.621	9,315
Net Present Value				-2,945

Workings:

Initial costs £57,000 + £8,000 removal of old system = £65,000

Net annual savings – years 1 and 2:
Energy £22,000 - £12,000; Maintenance £8,000 - £0; Depreciation ignored as non-cash item. Total annual savings £18,000

Net annual savings – years 3 to 5:
Energy £22,000 - £12,000; Maintenance £8,000 - £3,000; Depreciation ignored as non-cash item. Total annual savings £15,000

(b)   The net present value of the scheme is **negative**, so from a financial point of view the new boiler system is **not worthwhile**.

Task 2.4

Report on Scenarios

■   Contribution Amounts

The main reason for the difference in contributions is the pricing structure and anticipated room occupancy. The first scenario is based on an average price per room of £80 and an occupancy rate of 37.5%. The second scenario assumes a lower average price per room of £65, but a much higher occupancy rate of 75%. This increases the turnover of scenario 2 compared with scenario 1.

The variable costs of food and laundry are based on £10 and £7 per occupied room respectively under both scenarios. The cleaning cost per room is £12 under scenario 1, but reduced to £10 under scenario 2.

The combined impact of the above is a contribution amount under scenario 2 which is £375,000 greater than that shown in scenario 1.

■   Net Profit Margins and Amounts

The net profits arise from the contributions less the fixed costs. The only difference in fixed costs is selling and marketing where the second scenario anticipates spending £350,000 more. This is the cost of increased advertising and celebrity endorsement which it is anticipated will double the occupancy rate when combined with the reduced room prices.

The net profit amount is higher under the second scenario, although as a percentage of turnover it is lower (10.77% compared with 15.42%).

■   Recommendation, with reasons

Although the second scenario anticipates a higher net profit than scenario 1, it is only by a fairly small £25,000 difference. The second scenario relies on doubling room occupancy to 75%, and is therefore a more risky strategy. If this level of increased occupancy was not achieved there is scope for significantly reduced profit or even losses. The first scenario in contrast is based on current performance which is known to be achievable.

The recommendation is therefore to follow scenario 1.